A Nile Adventure

cruising and other stories

Kim Molyneaux

A Nile Adventure - cruising and other stories
First edition 2011

First Published USA, 2011

© Copyright Kim Molyneaux

All rights reserved. No part of this publication may be reproduced, stored in or introduced into a retrieval system, or transmitted, in any form, or by any means (electronic, mechanical, photocopying, recording or otherwise) without the prior written permission of the publisher.

This book is sold subject to the condition that it shall not, by way of trade or otherwise, be lent, resold, hired out, or otherwise circulated without the publisher's prior consent in any form of binding or cover other than that in which it is published and without a similar condition including this condition being imposed on the subsequent purchaser.

ISBN 978-1466327108

Printed by Create Space

Design and artwork by Kim Molyneaux – www.kimmolyneaux.com

Images © 2011 Kim Molyneaux

Foreword

by Wendy E Rose

I first met Kim Molyneaux when we ended up sitting next to each other at breakfast, dinner and tea on board a cruise ship on the River Nile in Egypt. As we had both been warned about the food and what to eat and what not to eat, our conversation with Kim and her family soon took off. It was fun comparing notes with them about what was nice to eat and then of course later on whether it had made us ill or not! We soon realised that the only problem with the food was that there was far too much of it!

When I realised Kim was keeping a journal of her travels, I was green with envy. But it was fun to sit by the pool and discuss how her journal was growing day by day! And now that I've read what she was writing I'm absolutely stunned by her accuracy. Kim has described the whole Nile experience and the trip to Hurghada superbly and her dry wit comes across in buckets full and makes me smile with a warm recognition of what a great time we had. Furthermore, Kim managed to absorb all the factual information that our guide was spilling out at a rapid rate of knots! She has also taken some extraordinary photographs; her clean sharp images jump out at you from the page.

My ambition is to write a novel just like my ancestor George Eliot, Mary Anne Evans. There is nothing more inspiring to the eyes and ears of a writer than a journey. So it was incredibly difficult for me to sit back and watch Kim write her journal about our holiday. I had, with regret, pledged not to pick up a pen or a laptop for a whole two weeks! Trained at the BBC as a journalist to write for the World Wide Web, I've written about everything from picking up litter at the roadside of the A14 to Eddie & The Hotrods. I have also broadcast on radio, producing and presenting my own programmes on 87.5 FM, and I have interviewed actors and politicians such as Patricia Routledge of *Keeping Up Appearances* fame and Robert Kilroy Silk, former chat show host come UKIP representative. Now much of my time is spent writing blogs, making video and commenting on social networking sites promoting musicians and their bands or small businesses. As a very smart, forward-looking woman, I often wonder what Mary Anne Evans would think to this very modern new way of writing in the fast-moving world of the 21st Century. Mind you, after viewing the hieroglyphics inside Ramses II tomb in the Valley of the Kings, I really do wonder what the Egyptian pharaohs would make of the World Wide Web!

I sincerely hope that Kim Molyneaux's *Nile Adventure* is a great success, whether it be in print on the shelf as a best seller or on the latest revolutionary reading gadgets available on the market. Whether she aspires as a writer to the success of the Pharaohs or George Eliot, this travel guide is a very great first and certainly not a last for Kim and I look forward to reading her next guide to a real world experience.

Wendy E Rose
www.wendyerose.com

Page 4

How this book works

I have gathered together all the information that I should/would/could (or in my case, couldn't) have known before, during and after our Nile cruise and presented it here in a light-hearted story.

The histories of the monuments are short and simplified. They are not intended to be a substitute for anything produced by our learned historians – just easier to digest.

The sections are as follows:

- **Tips** concerning key aspects of the trip which it would be useful to know before you go.

- **Brief, easy-to-digest histories** of the temples and monuments we visited.

- **Occasional menus** to whet your appetite. In our cruise package, all food served at breakfast, lunch and dinner was included, as was afternoon tea served on sailing days (and only sailing days, mind). All drinks had to be paid for. Our hotel package was 'all inclusive', unless you wanted a bottle of wine!

- There's the **light-hearted story of our journey and adventures** to the wonderful world of ancient and modern Egypt, which can be used to while away all your lazy afternoons on board.

- **Photographs**, strategically placed adjacent to the relevant text to bring it to life.

Even if you are not planning a Nile cruise, I hope you will find my story interesting and entertaining – take a virtual trip!

Contents

Foreword by Wendy E Rose 3
How this book works 7
Introduction 11
Itinerary 12
Map 15
Timeline 16
Optional excursions 18
Tuesday 5th July - Travel day from Geneva to Gatwick 19
Tip - Budget before you go 22
Wednesday 6 July - Travel day from Gatwick to Luxor 23
Dinner menu 28
Thursday 6 July - Kom Ombo Temple 31
Lunch menu 32
History - Kom Ombo Temple 38
Friday 8 July - Philae Temple 41
Tip - Buying souvenirs 44
Lunch menu 47
Nile Adventure 49
History - Philae Temple 54
The Rosetta Stone 58
Dinner menu 59
Saturday 9th July - Aswan 61
Tip - Aswan Market 66
History - The cartouche 68
History - Abu Simbel 70
Sunday 10th July - Edfu Temple 73
Lunch menu 76
History - Edfu Temple 82
Monday 11th July - visit to the West Bank 85
Tip - Valley of the Kings and Valley of the Queens 86
Tombs in the Valley of the Kings 90
Tricking the grave robbers 92
The curse of the tombs 93

Page 8

History - Valley of the Kings 94
History - Mortuary Temple of Queen Hot Chicken Soup 100
History - Habu Temple 106
History - Colossi of Memnon 108
Tuesday 12th July - Karnak Complex and Luxor Temple 111
Tip - On board 119
History - Karnak Complex 120
History - Luxor Temple 122
Tip - Cruising 124
Lunch menu 125
Wednesday 13th July - Luxor to Hurghada 127
Hotel menu 134
Thursday 14th July - Day in the hotel at Hurghada 135
Friday 15th July - Travel day from Hurghada to Gatwick 141
Hotel facilities 142
Towel sculptures 146
Useful Arabic words 148
Acknowledgements 149
References 150
About the author 151

Introduction

Travelling to Egypt as a family was both exciting and daunting at the same time. Hours of painstaking research went into the wonders we would be visiting, and, a few ink cartridges later, voila! Our DIY Nile Cruise Manual, all neatly arranged in order, which, of course, got more and more messed up as the week went on.

During my research, I was overwhelmed with fascinating stories about ancient Egypt and couldn't wait to jump in but where was all the practical information specific to a cruise? Why couldn't I find everything I wanted to know all together in one place? Wouldn't it be great to find descriptions of the monuments and an idea of what to expect on board easily?!

I decided to write this journal, not only because I thought I would enjoy doing it (which I did – it's been really good fun!) but also, I hoped it would be useful for future travellers to be a bit more clued-up and so better prepared for their journey and experience. So now, here it is, is lots of useful information, conveniently all together – an honest travel guide and a real-life account of the whole journey in one.

This book is specifically about our Nile cruise and our brief stay in Hurghada in July, 2011. All cruise itineraries vary slightly, however, if you've booked the full excursion package, you will get to visit all the main temples and tombs.

Itinerary

Tuesday 5 July
Fly from Geneva to Gatwick

Wednesday 6 July
Fly from Gatwick to Luxor
Transfer to cruise ship
Overnight in Luxor

Thursday 7 July
Cruise and afternoon visit to Kom Ombo Temple
Overnight in Aswan
Evening Nubian dancing show

Friday 8 July
Morning visit to Philae Temple by coach and motorboat
with felluca ride
Optional afternoon Nile Adventure trip

Saturday 9 July
Optional visit to Abu Simbel Temple by coach
Cruise and overnight in Edfu
Evening on board Egyptian party

Sunday 10 July
Morning visit to Edfu Temple by horse-drawn carriage
Cruise and overnight in Luxor

Monday 11 July
Morning visit to the West Bank to the Valley of the Kings,
Valley of the Queens, Habu Temple and Colossi of Memnon
Optional evening sound and light show in Luxor
Overnight in Luxor

Tuesday 12 July
Optional early morning hot air balloon ride
Morning visit to Karnak Complex and Luxor Temple
Optional afternoon city tour of Luxor
by horse drawn carriage
Evening Egyptian dancing show

Wednesday 13 July
Morning taxi ride from Luxor to Hurghada
Afternoon in Hurghada

Thursday 14 July
Day at the hotel in Hurghada

Friday 15 July
Morning in Hurghada
Late afternoon flight from Hurghada to Gatwick

Saturday 16, Sunday 17 July
Visit family and stocking up on supplies in the UK

Monday 18 July
Flight from Gatwick to Geneva

this is our 'Full Excursion' package

Exchange rates July 2011

UK£1 = LE 9.70
€1 = LE 8.60
US$1 = LE 5.95

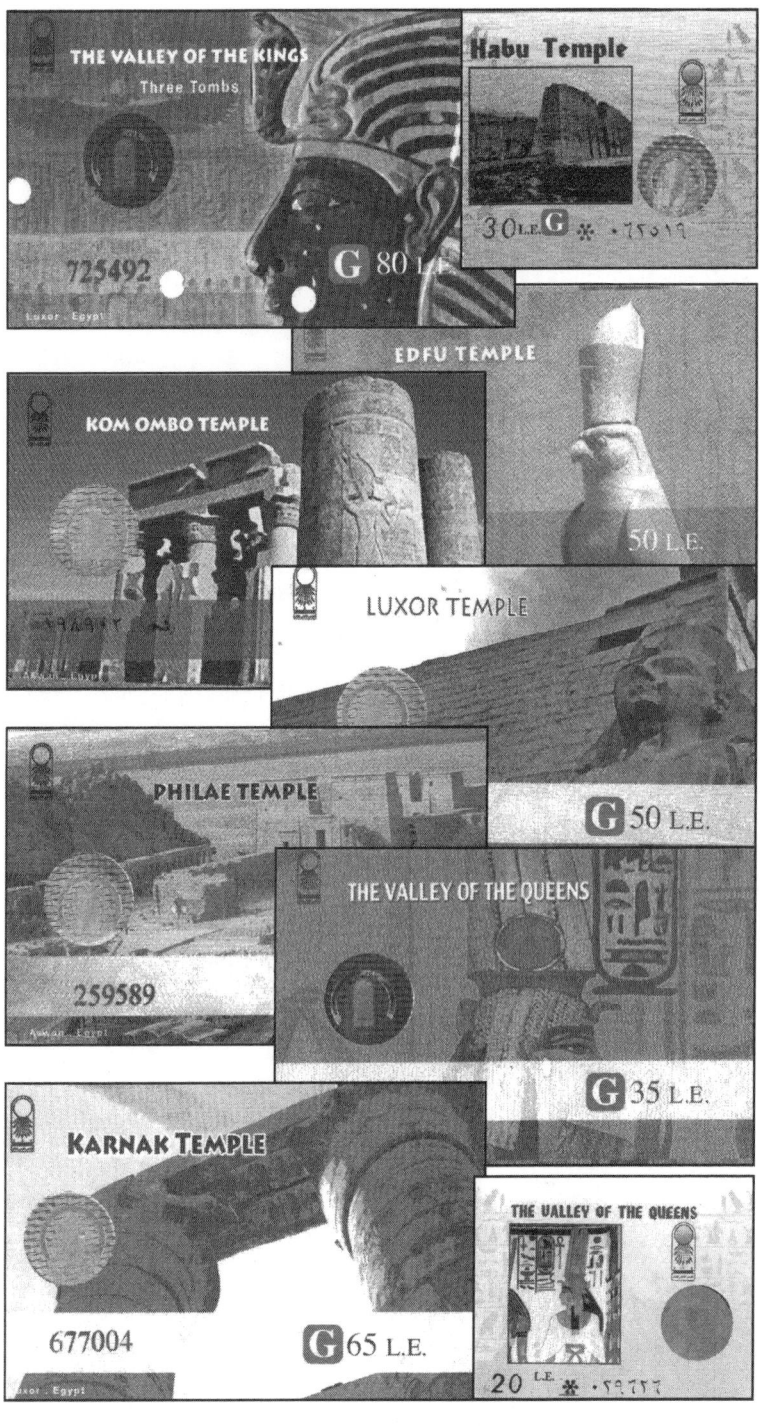

Map

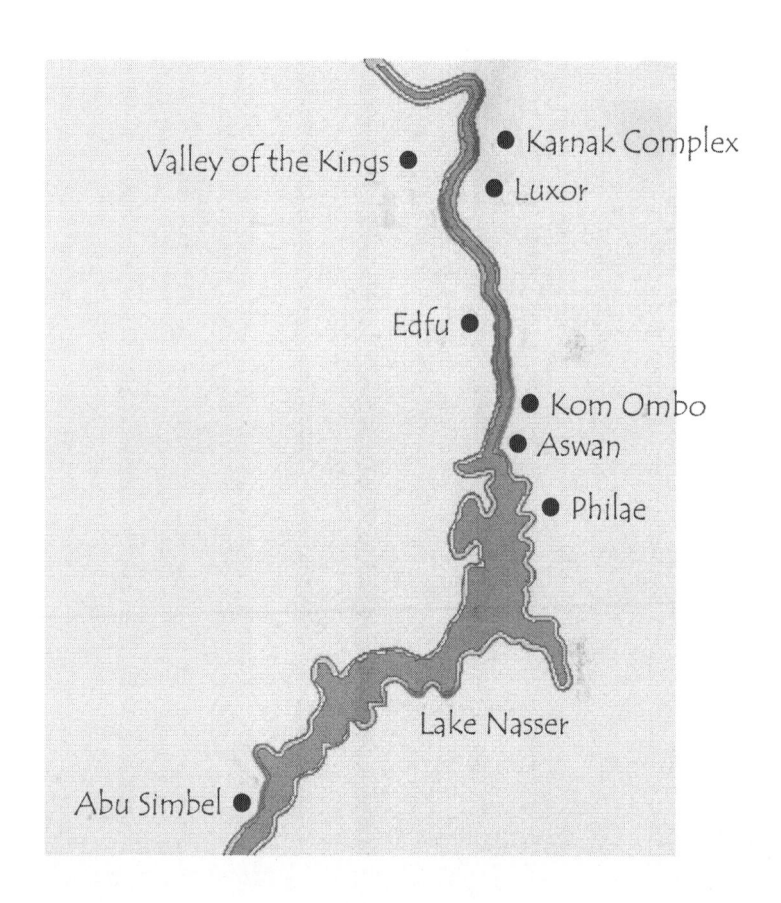

Timeline

3100 BC King Menes founded the **1st Dynasty**

3100-2950 BC **1st and 2nd Dynasties** ruled
Introduction of hieroglyphics
Memphis established as the capital

2950-2575 BC **3rd Dynasty**
King Djosa built the first Step Pyramid
at Saqqara

2575 -2150 BC **The Old Kingdom** (4th-8th Dynasties)
The Great Pyramids were built at Dahshur
and Giza

2125-1975 BC **1st Intermediate Period**
(9th-11th Dynasties)
Book of the Dead created

1975-1640 BC **The Middle Kingdom**
(11th-14th Dynasties)
Amenemhet overthrew Mentuhotep III
Upper and Lower Egypt reunited
Thebes becomes the capital

1630 -1520 BC **2nd Intermediate Period**
(15th-17th Dynasties)

1539 -1075 BC **New Kingdom** (18th-20th Dynasties)
Building of the tombs of the Valley of Kings
and Karnak
The great Pharaohs included Hatshepsut,
Akhenaten, Tutankhamun, Tuthmosis and
Ramses II
Ramses XI was the last of the rulers of
the New Kingdom
Capital moves to Memphis

1075-715 BC	3rd Intermediate Period (21st-25th Dynasties)
715-332 BC	The Late Period (20th-30th Dynasties)
332 BC	Alexander the Great conquers Egypt His general, Ptolemy, becomes king
196 BC	The Rosetta Stone is carved
51-30 BC	**Cleopatra VII reigns** becomes the mistress of Julius Caesar and gives birth to their son, Octavian
37 BC	Queen Cleopatra VII of the Ptolemies marries Mark Antony
31 BC	Octavian defeats Antony and Cleopatra in the sea Battle of Actium. Both Antony and Cleopatra commit suicide
30 BC	Egypt becomes a province of the Roman Empire
384 AD	Theodosius orders the adherence to Christianity

Nile Adventure - £20
Visit to Lord Kitchener's Botanical Gardens by motorboat
Visit to a Nubian village
with optional camel ride £7

Abu Simbel - £65
by coach (with bathroom), leaving at 4am

Sound and light show at Karnak - £25

Hot air balloon trip over Luxor
in the early morning - £80

City tour of Luxor by caleche - £10

All these activities you can book independently yourself at slightly lower prices, but with hindsight, it was much easier for us to go on organised visits, as you'll see later

Prices per person in UK £s (children under 12 half price)

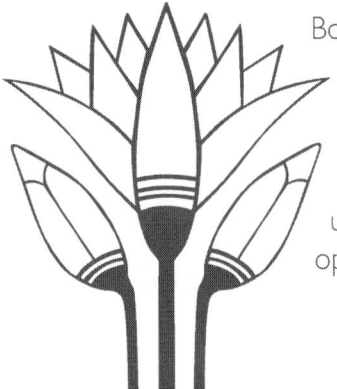

Booking the **Full Excursion Package** in advance with your agent is usually cheaper than booking the equivalent excursions on board. It is unlikely to include any of these optional excursions listed above

Optional Excursions

Tuesday 5th July

Travel day from Geneva to Gatwick

Thoroughly excited about our journey ahead, after an early lunch we left for Geneva Airport. Our Nile adventure was something we had long been looking forward to with eager anticipation. This, for us, was a holiday of a lifetime! (I forgot to mention, we live in Switzerland.)

Everything went to plan – parking: no problem; checked in OK. Thankfully our eldest daughter (15 going on 25) had decided not to wear her giant metal-studded belt that's guaranteed to set airport security doors howling. We bought slices of delicious quiches for lunch and even boarded almost on time!

First stop, Gatwick Airport. Having collected our luggage after the customary wait for the conveyor belt number, off we went to look for our bus stop. We'd booked a family room at the Gatwick Travelodge for the night as our Luxor flight left early next morning. As it had only cost £19, we were expecting to 'rough it' a bit, not, as you will see, endure the almost complete nightmare it turned out to be!

There was major construction going on at Gatwick 'for our ultimate enjoyment of an improved airport', which meant quite a trek to find bus stop number 7, and, with 10 minutes to spare, we rushed through the rain in what we were pretty sure was the right direction. It was, and it was mostly covered, but the bus was 20 minutes late, of course. Good news – it was less expensive than advertised! (£6 for the family instead of £10.) When we got off the bus – horror! We had stayed at this Travelodge before and had faithfully promised ourselves never to do so again – must make notes in future!

Well, we're here now, we've paid our £19 and here we stay – except the air conditioning was blowing out warm air and the windows were all sealed shut! Ken (hubby) disappeared and reappeared with the lady from the reception desk, who was extremely bubbly and friendly. She pressed a few buttons and sighed. "Only a few parts of the hotel have functioning aircon," she told us. "I'll find you another room."

We went for a drink in the bar. Finding something for Melody (7), our youngest, to drink was a bit of a challenge. She doesn't do fizzy drinks and eventually settled for orange juice.

Mrs Bubbly returned with a big smile and a new card key. She'd even moved the girls' bedding for us and found me an extra pillow.

I couldn't fault the service, even if the building wasn't up to scratch. We spoke with the manager who explained she'd just taken over the job the day before and was determined to transform the hotel into a nice place to stay. There was a chance this is a standard excuse she gives to anyone who complains, but on the other hand, she could well have been completely genuine and the next time we make the 'fatal' mistake of booking that particular Travelodge, we'll be pleasantly surprised – fingers crossed!

The new room was nice and cool. We carefully avoided the black marks around the bath and covered up the sharp bed-side shelf at child-head height with a pillow, but were morally obliged to point out the water dripping out of the electrical socket in the bathroom!

Luckily, we had had the foresight to pack an emergency bottle of wine. Ellen, our eldest, who, although I'm biased, is a bit of a head-turner, did a great job in getting four pint glasses full of ice cubes from the bar and the rubbish bin made an absolutely perfect wine cooler!

Our two tired girls lay down to sleep on the pull-out sofa. Ellen had been ill and went to sleep straight away. Melody proved more difficult, as usual. I came back from the bathroom to find she'd jumped into my bed! Monster! I got into hers and pretended to go to sleep. As soon as she had drifted off, Ken grabbed her legs and with me at the head end, we swapped her back into her bed, using a well-practised swing manoeuvre. We tried to watch one of the four available TV channels (in silence) – seriously bad reception. Given there wasn't much else to look at, it was most amusing to see black lines going up and down and from side to side. Where would they come from next? Then they were gone, and then they were back again! Thank goodness for that nice, cold bottle of wine!

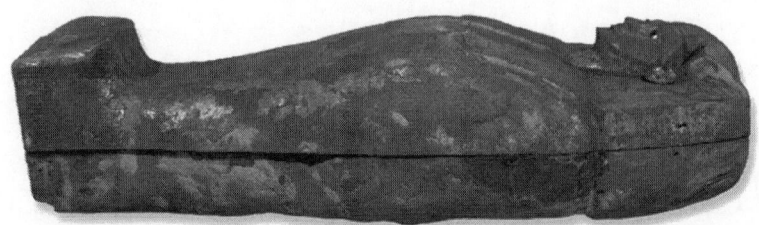

Budget before you go

Tourist Visa - £25 per couple (two children count as a couple). Get it at the airport when you arrive.

Baqsheesh (tips) are a way of life in Egypt. It's part of the culture. Everyone who does anything at all for you, whether you wanted them to or not, will expect one. Their favourites are £2 coins, but they are happy with a £1 coin. Get hold of a handful of LE1 coins to give away – the equivalent of about 10 English pence (10p).

Beware - the LE10 note looks very similar to the 10 Piaster note (worth about 10p) - easy to switch in the market without you realising!

Ship Staff Baqsheesh - we were asked for £15 per person (in cash, half price for children under 12) which would be shared out between ship staff members, so it would not be necessary to tip them individually. Some of the really helpful staff we gave extra tips to. To ensure he received an additional 'thank you', one waiter gave us a 'gift' of nuts and dried hibiscus leaves!

Optional Excursions - Prices we paid are on page 12.

Tip

Wednesday 6 July
Travel day from Gatwick to Luxor

Up at 5.30am (usual time for us as the UK is an hour behind Switzerland). Giggling, the girls recounted the story of Melody getting into bed with Ellen in the middle of the night and laying sprawled out, while Ellen was squished against the wall – well, if you are going to sleep walk, it may as well be to somewhere comfy! Ken and I had slept through the whole thing and hadn't heard a peep, despite only being a metre away (the wine or the hypnotic effect of the TV)?

All packed, we left this wonderful hotel, caught the bus back to the construction site which was so much improved on yesterday I thoroughly enjoyed it, and raided M&S for lunch. Even EasyJet to Luxor only offers cheese toasties, bacon butties and Pringles for sustenance.

Everything seemed on time. We chatted to a seasoned Egypt visitor in the boarding queue who advised Ellen to tie her blond hair up or she would be just too popular with the locals (this happens to her wherever we are, she should be used to it by now). This particular lady was very friendly and lamented how much things had changed in Luxor since she had started visiting many years ago. Apparently there were now paving slabs in the souk rather than mud and it is covered to give

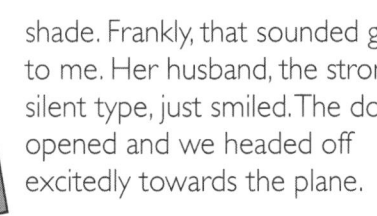

shade. Frankly, that sounded good to me. Her husband, the strong, silent type, just smiled. The door opened and we headed off excitedly towards the plane.

On board, there was a suspicious lack of the usual EasyJet-style urgency. It turned out there was a 45 minute delay for a take-off slot – so I here I am writing this entry.

Finally taxiing away from the terminal, the sun came out and Ellen read about the last Harry Potter film which would be released the day we were due to land back in the UK. "Can we go, Mum..? Can we...? Please?" She did get to see it, but not until we had returned home.

The plane journey was, well, a plane journey. Long and a bit boring, punctuated by entertaining snatches eavesdropping on other people's conversations. The girls occupied themselves playing Nintendo DS and reading Cressida Cowell. Most of the other passengers were, like us, in a state of eager anticipation.

The pilot took some short cuts (how?) and with a following wind, we made the journey in about four-and-a-half hours, arriving around 5pm (Egypt was one hour ahead of the UK so there we were, back in our habitual time zone).

Flying over Greece was interesting – fun to see the islands and try to guess which one was which. When we reached the Egyptian coastline, I was very excited, thinking I'd seen old Roman mosaics. In fact, it was a small housing complex – what a disappointment (and how daft can you get)!

Luxor airport is modern and clean. A bus ride took us to the arrivals hall where we found a row of guys shaking plaques with names on. (There is a distinct lack of women working throughout Egypt.) Finding our name, we were taken to a desk to have visas stuck in our passports. "Pay for them on the bus," we were told. £25 cash per couple. Can't blame them for putting the price up, given the current exchange rates. Our visas were stamped by the guard at the desk and then double checked by the next guard in a flash white uniform sitting only two metres away who had very carefully watched them being stamped!

In the ladies', which was completely up to date, clean and extremely well-appointed in brown marble, the attendant held out her hand (note: token woman!) displaying a row of £1 coins. She asked me if I could change them for a £10 note (I think). I didn't have any, so wasn't able to help her. I lost count of the number of times we were asked this in the week that followed. Realising everyone would now be expecting tips (baqsheesh), I slipped some coins into my back pocket – just to be prepared.

With our cases in tow, we left the cool interior of the airport, emerging into the hot, sultry, late afternoon heat. Wow!

Our guide collected our small group together, ushering us all in the right direction in an efficient, guidly-like fashion. As we were walking from the airport to the transfer coach, several men came running towards us, hoping to pull our cases for a tip. A polite 'no, thank you' did the trick. The guys loading the cases onto the coach, however, pointedly held out their hands. Ha! I was 20p worse off!

There were a lot of ships docked at Luxor itself. Ours, as it turned out, was in the new dock, about 6 miles out of town. The coach drove through the streets – bougainvillea-lined roads with an attendant every few hundred metres trimming the beautiful flowers. We passed people walking in the roads (no pavements in sight here), men with their wives or children on the back of mopeds, donkey-drawn carriages with piles of hay on the back and the tourist caleches waiting for business, not to mention numerous blue and white taxis.

Beeeep went the coach horn, every time we approached a pedestrian or a vehicle, despite the 'no horn' signs every 20 metres. We passed row upon row of ship embarkation bays, each with its own gate attendant beckoning us to come in!

Arriving at our dock, the very smartly dressed gate attendant who could have been the captain himself, leisurely lifted the barrier. In front of us was the Champollion I – very impressive! Next to it was the much smaller and shabbier Sun Azur with another three ships docked directly behind her. Guess which one we were booked on?

Our guide, Akil, puffed out his chest and proudly announced we had all been upgraded, free of charge, to the 5 star Champollion – result! Funny, the Sun Azur had been listed as 5 stars, too. Her poor stars must have been faded and distant compared with her shining counterpart moored alongside.

There's no denying it. This is a very nice ship. I imagined it was the bee's knees in the 1950s, as that was the era the decor appeared to be from. I later found out she was built in 1993! The entrance boasts a magnificent marble staircase, fit for Scarlet O'Hara in her long red velvet gown to make her entrance! Our newly-acquainted group of ship-mates was led to the bar while the bell boys unloaded our cases from the coach and we were offered a delicious hibiscus juice drink, wonderfully cold. We filled in our registration cards. Well, I did, Ken had his contacts in and couldn't see a thing!

It was pretty dark in this sumptuously-decorated, circular room. It was cool and came complete with a central stage surrounded by ebony pillars and luxurious sofas all around.

The guide collected our cards and announced our upgrade from a lower deck cabin to the middle deck – double result! Not only that, they had they given us a double room with interconnecting door to a twin room for the girls. Perfect!

The rooms were decorated in an elegant fashion of a bygone era, delightful with walnut headboards and cabinets and gilded mirrors. Only drawback – no toilet paper can be put down the loo – à la Greque. The girls were thrilled and set about unpacking. I'd helpfully mixed all our belongings together in case we lost a suitcase en route, so it was a bit of a free for all. The temperature had not quite reached the dizzy heights I was expecting, although the struggling air con did make the rooms a little sticky. Maybe it would improve once we set sail (we hoped!), so we abandoned the packing and headed for the sun deck.

Up on the top deck of the ship with the warm breeze blowing

Dinner Menu

Pumpkin soup and selection of breads

Filo pastry triangle filled with delicious cream cheese

Salad – tomatoes, cabbage, carrots, olives – everyone on our table refused to eat it except us, believing it may have been washed in local water. We later found out they wash everything in mineral water so we lived to tell the tale!

Dish of hummus

Steak, rice, green beans

Pancakes covered in chocolate sauce and Chantilly cream with a glacé cherry

around, we were surprised to see the sun set so early, around 7.30pm. The girls paddled in the shallow surround of the pool as I snapped away at the breathtakingly beautiful golden sunset.

Little did I know how accustomed I would become to opening that door to the sun deck at the top of the stairs, only to be hit by the relentless heat of the day.

Dinner on board is served at 8pm. A candle-lit, silver service affair – pretty dark – we wondered if they were trying to hide the food! We needn't have worried.

The girls picked out the bits they thought they would like. The adults ate a bit of everything, it was all very tempting. We wondered what our waistlines would look like at the end of the week if we continued eating like this!

Our table companions were two English couples. Wendy and Colin, from a charming little thatched village near Cambridge which still had all its amenities (post office, bank and three pubs) and Sally and George from the Midlands. Sometimes the nicest people say the funniest things – Sally and George were on their second Egyptian foray. They entertained

us with the story of when they had been taken out into the desert to share a meal with a Bedouin tribe and watch the sunset. The meal was delicious and the sunset was spectacular, after which they had to be taken home in the dark. Our intrepid travellers had no idea how the Bedouin had managed to guide them home through the desert in the dark without a GPS system! How wonderful!

We dutifully signed for our drinks, which was a surprise as we had expected them to be included, and retired for the night. Despite their over-tiredness, the girls insisted on playing DS before going to sleep. It wasn't long before their room quietened down.

The ship had set sail during dinner. The sensation was, well, non-existent. There was a slight rumble on the lower deck (dining room level) but that was it. I was amazed. Boats and I don't generally make good travelling companions. I'd kept my fears to myself, determined to enjoy myself, whatever and was thoroughly relieved I would not be needing my secret stash of travel pills. Cross-channel ferries had always been a nightmare for me ever since I can remember. I once went on the Isle of Wight ferry and just about felt OK. It was soon after my mum passed away and my sister reckoned our mum had passed on her sea legs to me. Maybe she was right. Thanks, Mum!

I didn't sleep much the first night. We were thrilled to get a king-sized bed, although it was slightly harder than we were used to and the imprint of the previous occupants laid testament to the fact that they had slept as far away from their bed partners as possible, making snuggling up a bit uncomfortable, to say the least! (It was too hot, anyway.)

Thursday 6 July
Cruise and afternoon visit to Kom Ombo Temple

I woke early desperately in need of a bottle of mineral water. I should have arranged to have one the night before as it's recommended you don't even clean your teeth in the local stuff. There were a couple of men swilling the entrance floor in a pool of soapy water. There was no passing that! The bar and restaurant were closed until 8am and not a waiter in sight, so I was stymied. Everyone got dressed and went up to the sun deck to wait and absorb the early morning warmth.

Breakfast consisted of tea and coffee, a selection of hot meals including spiced sausage, onion and spicy peppers, mashed potatoes and mini croissants. Egg Chef showed off his dexterity with a pan in each hand while he cooked our omelettes and scrambled egg in front of us. Cereal, plain yoghurt, jam, honey, different breads, cakes and pastries, cheese, olives and tomatoes made up the cold breakfast. The selection was pretty much the same each morning.

I went back to our cabin to find it had already been cleaned and tidied. New towels had been 'sculpted' in the shape of two kissing swans and had been artistically arranged on our beds. What a lovely touch. I didn't tell the girls – I was looking forward to seeing their surprised and delighted faces.

Lunch Menu

Clear soup with chick peas, lentils and pulses
and a selection of breads

Courgettes, peppers and aubergines stuffed with rice

Fresh salad, tomato, chillies, cucumber
and tatziki salad

Roast chicken breast stuffed with rice (and more rice) –
Melody was thrilled,
chicken is her favourite at the moment

Spiced tomato and potato slices with fish tagine
(particularly excellent)

Buffet of fresh fruit
(figs, melon, oranges, grapes, green bananas)
and chocolate-topped sponge cake

check out the cow in the boat

We spent the morning on the sun deck, sunbathing, shadebathing and paddling in the pool. It was a tad hot, to say the least.

Groups of children shouted "Hello" at us from the banks of the Nile, occasionally. A group of our fellow passengers turned out to be a very pleasant Arabic-speaking family from London. Their son, who had just sat his GCSEs, chuckled and told us that the 'hello' was followed by some colourful Arabic expletives!

Lunch – I decided to be a bit more selective about what I actually ate at meal times. The food was fab but there was just too much. Lunch? More like a great feast!

Sitting on deck, I still had to look up at the passing landscape to reassure myself I was really on a moving ship. Miles and miles of river bank went by, mostly palms and rocks with a few ruins thrown in, until, at about 4pm, there were signs of civilization ahead.

Our first official excursion: Kom Ombo Temple. We docked at the end of the 'harbour' around 5pm. Approaching, it had been quite a relief to see a tall chimney and buildings appearing on the horizon after hours of deserted countryside. It was still very warm and breezy.

I was the first off the ship: bad idea, never do that again! I was first in line for the street sellers. We were led up the majestic stairs to the temple and listened intently to Akil's fascinating description while trying to find little patches of shade to shelter in. After his talk, we were free to wander around the ruins for a while, taking photos and trying to decipher the hieroglyphics. We marvelled at the columns and the walls around the entrance hall and all the inner chambers. The fabulous sun set caught up with us as we made our way back to the ship.

There were hardly any tourists, which could not be said of the street sellers – they were out in force, shaking shawls and scarves at us before we even docked! "Lady, lady, very nice hat, very good quality, very cheap!" The scarves were nice. What I hadn't realised was that the prices were in English pounds, not Egyptian. I nearly got a bargain scarf until I realised my mistake and was relentlessly hounded all the way back to the ship. These guys could win awards for persistency! They tried to sell things as if their lives depended on it, which, actually, they probably did. The scarf was repeatedly thrown over my shoulder, despite my attempts

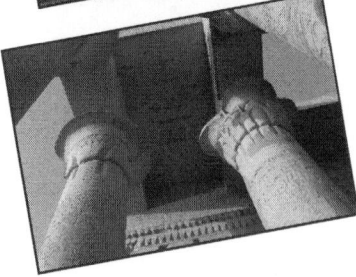

to give it back. The price varied with every step – upwards and downwards. Eventually I could have bought it for LE80 (probably could have at home, too) but I'd found the hassle so overwhelming my stubborn streak struck out and that was it – I was not buying anything, no matter what. So, I left without my scarf.

Melody was looking for an Egyptian dress for Saturday night's party; not that we had any intention of going to the party – it started far too late for a little girl to stay up, but it was nice for her to have the dress, anyway. She'd seen one in the little ship's shop which was bright pink with Nefertiri on the front, resplendent in beads and sequins – a little girl's dream! We were sure we would find a suitable dress on shore, probably cheaper and were certain that the street sellers needed the money more than the shipping line. The street sellers had little 'shops' of their own along the waterfront – little square tented affairs with open fronts, their wares waving around in the warm breeze, and their owners tried to interest her in a selection of different dresses. They had blue, burgundy, white, but nothing matched up to the vision of the little pink number

on board. Unfortunately for them, there was no sale. No choice but to go straight back to the ship's shop for a fitting. It was perfect – sold to the little girl (the only one on the ship by the way, so she had a great fuss made of her) for LE70. Chike, who was in charge of souvenirs and jewellery sales on board, wouldn't take our money just then. He insisted he would give us a 'good price' for the other three costumes he was hoping to sell to the rest of our family for the party on Saturday. I didn't tell him it was highly unlikely he would get any further sales from us. I couldn't imagine being able to persuade Ken and Ellen into such a costume – no way!

We set sail for Aswan shortly after embarkation and went to change for dinner which, this evening, was to be served on the sun deck.

Arriving in good time, the sun deck was wafted with the perpetual warm breeze. Despite the darkness, Melody decided she wanted to sit right by the railings. There probably wouldn't have been any problem; I didn't really have any fears of her falling over the side, her chin just about touched the top railing, but it niggled me all the same. Asking if we could sit at one of the middle tables practically caused a riot! No!

We had been allocated a group table, and at that group table we were obliged to sit throughout the whole voyage! We settled on the farthest table, which at least had a colourful screen tied from the roof to the railings, to add to the atmosphere. Our fellow table guests were equally surprised by the restriction and agreed it would have been nice to get to know other guests over dinner. However, as it turned out, we all got along very well and some of the other guests were not that desirable, after all!

Tonight there was a buffet, a choice of salads, soup and hot dishes – beautifully tender beef chunks, fish and even a special kind of lasagne with pasta on top and rice underneath. Pudding, amongst other things, was jelly – guess who was first in line for that!

We ate our meal watching little lights on the bank slowly pass us by. The girls were bored with the adult conversation and went to paddle in the pool. Eventually they went down to the cabin to find a surprise 'elephant' awaited them on the bed. The staff were indeed expert towel artists! They'd even put sunglasses and hats on them! This ritual became a source of daily delight – anticipating what innovative 'sculpture' we would find the following day.

Kom Ombo

Kom Ombo stands serenely, overlooking the Nile, just south of Gebel el-Silsila, between Aswan and Edfu. Situated on the ancient caravan route between the heart of Egypt and the gold mines of the Eastern Desert, it used to be a resting stop for conquering armies, amongst other things.

This temple is unusual in that it is a double temple, with one side dedicated to the god Haroesis and the other to Sobek. The design is almost perfectly symmetrical.

The left side is dedicated to Haroeris, the 'Good Doctor' (a form of the falcon-headed god Horus the Elder) along with his consort Ta-Sent-Nefer, the 'Good Sister' (a form of Hathor).

The right side is dedicated to Sobek-Re (the crocodile god combined with the sun god Re), along with his wife (another form of Hathor) and their son Khonsu-Hor. Sobek is associated with Seth, who was the enemy of Horus. In the myth of Horus and Osiris, Seth and his followers changed themselves into crocodiles to escape.

There are no crocodiles in this part of the Nile today, however, at the time, this bend in the river was a favoured spot for them to bask in the sun and snap at the locals. The ancient Egyptians believed that by honouring the fearsome crocodile as a god, they would be safe from attacks. A small pool nearby was used for raising sacred crocodiles. In the Chapel of Hathor near the entrance, there are three crocodile mummies, which were uncovered during nearby roadworks in the 1970s.

The temple complex was built over a period spanning more than 400 years, first started by the Ptolemies in the 2nd

Century BC and finally completed by the Romans in 218AD (in particular, Emperor Trajan). Then, over the centuries, stones were removed to be used in buildings elsewhere and earthquakes left the site in ruins. Nile flood silt deposits and fierce desert sandstorms virtually buried it.

The main temple at Kom Ombo was originally cleared of debris by Jacques de Morgan in 1893. By that time, the temple's Grand Pylon (ceremonial gateway) was lost. However, the archaeologists were able to resurrect other parts, especially the stunning entrance-way and outer Hypostyle hall.

One of the most striking reliefs in the temple shows an offering of medical equipment to the deified Imhotep, architect of the step pyramid at Saqqara. This relief dates to the end of the 2nd Century AD and shows a remarkably high level of medical technology, with tweezers, forceps and various other modern-looking utensils clearly visible.

At the entrance of Kom Ombo Temple, many of the larger columns have remained intact, adorned with pictures of serpents, birds, fruits and surgical tools. Larger than life depictions of Sobek and Haroeris, in addition to other gods such as Horus, cover the columns and the corridor walls. Some colours can still be seen on some of the columns. One in particular is well-preserved. No one can offer an explanation as to why the colours on this particular column have survived.

Today, Kom Ombo is home to many Nubians who were displaced from their ancestral homes by the rise of Lake Nasser caused by the Aswan Dam. Tourism is not the only industry in Kom Ombo: sugar cane is harvested on the river banks and there are felucca-building yards here.

Entrance price: adults LE30, children LE15

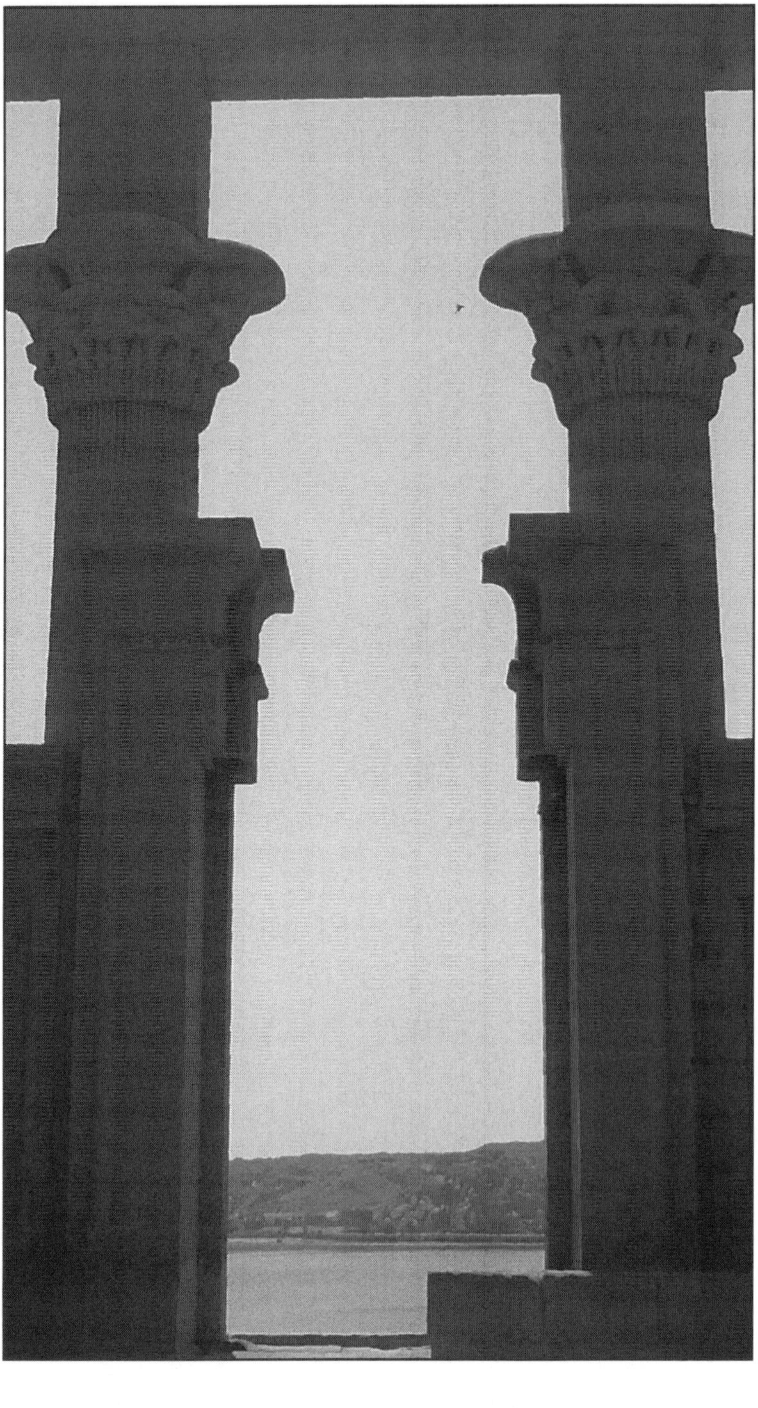

Friday 8 July

Morning visit to Philae Temple
by coach and motorboat, followed by felucca ride
Optional afternoon Nile Adventure trip

A 6am wake-up call found us all up and ready to hit the dining room for breakfast. I 'stole' a few bread rolls for our excursion this morning, just in case!

We were off to Philae Temple, dedicated to Isis – goddess of love. In its original location, Philae Temple was flooded for many months of the year due to the construction of the Aswan Dam. It was moved to the nearby island of Agilika thanks to a UNESCO project between 1972 and 1980.

Our coach pulled up at the waterside and we descended, walking along a little jetty and we boarded one of the awaiting motor boats. There was a small Nubian village on the banks high above us to admire while the captain manoeuvred us a little way out into the water and then stopped the noisy engine so we could listen to Akil's explanations. The crew were selling pretty necklaces and trinkets on the way for an English pound or two each.

It was extremely hot. The few tourist groups around were standing in the shade to listen to their guides and marvel at the impressive surroundings. After a further explanation of the history of the temple, we had a short while to look around on our own and take more photographs.

Brief History, according to our guide

Isis was married to Osiris (the goody), who was hated by his own brother, Seth (the baddy). Everyone wanted Osiris to be their king (except Seth, of course), and Seth 'killed' Osiris by tricking him into a coffin, then having his cronies dump the coffin in the river. Luckily Isis found him and brought him back to life by magic and they went back to live in Philae Temple. At some length, Seth found out that his plan had backfired and managed to trap Osiris again. He decided the only way to ensure Osiris stayed dead was to chop him up into little bits and distribute his body parts around. At the time, mummification was considered a vital part of passing into the next world, so with the help of another god, Isis transformed into an eagle and flew around to find her husband's bits and pieces so she could put him back together to be mummified. She found everything apart from his manly parts which were reputedly fed to the crocodiles. Their son, Horus, was miraculously conceived despite the missing vital equipment. That's much more succinct and easy to digest than anything I found on the web!

The café at the temple sells drinks and ice creams. Here we found little stalls selling souvenirs (a bit dusty, but not the end of the world). I can recommend buying what you want in places like this, even if it is slightly more expensive. There was absolutely no hassle – it's infinitely less stressful than facing the charge of the Light Brigade, unless you like that sort of thing, of course. We sat on thick-cushioned chairs, under the shady trees, next to enormous fans spraying cooling water at us, drinking nice, cold refreshing drinks – the ice creams were melting too quickly to eat!

There were a few Egyptian men, traditionally dressed, hanging around the temple. They would ask if you wanted your photo taken, either with or without them, in return for a coin or two, or notes, preferably. We managed to avoid them, leaving others the pleasure of this interaction.

Next stop, the perfume factory. What can I say – it was pretty pungent! Some of the aromas were better than others. I'm a bad judge as I can't smell very well at the best of times but these scents certainly got through, even to me! We enjoyed a talk and a 'smelling'. Their 'Five Secrets' perfume, they

Buying souvenirs

We found that the guide has a great relationship with the places he took us to. Even if you don't have the cash or camels to pay for whatever you want on you, he can arrange for you to take your goodies away and pay for them on the ship by all the usual methods - Egyptian Pounds, Euros, English Pounds, US Dollars or credit card. Obviously he gets a cut of every sale, paid for immediately or not. The visits were slick and well-organised, so we thought he deserved it.

...and another completely unrelated tip:

take a can of fly spray with you - you may find it useful!

Tip

In the perfume shop there were toilets, but no paper

informed us, was the base of Channel No. 5, and 'Aida' was the base for Opium. The list was extensive, to say the least.

The shop displayed a whole array of beautiful glass bottles to store the perfumes in, hand-made and painted with gold at around LE120 each. I treated myself to a very delicate bottle which was carefully wrapped for me and placed in a little box. The girls bought some perfume and were very happy to have 'real' scent.

We waited outside for one or two of our fellow tourists who couldn't quite decide whether to buy the Aida or the Lotus Flower perfume. Others came out with bags full of essential oils that would cure their digestive disorders, skin complaints and arthritis. Good luck to them!

Bag and bead sellers tried to tempt us in the few steps from the door to the coach. One, even, was a woman – first time I had seen that.

Felucca sailing. For our final treat of the morning, we boarded a felucca to take us back to the ship for lunch. Such a wonderful contraption with little or no means of steering. The boat weaved this way and that, the sail was raised, then lowered again. The crew rushed to stop us colliding with various adjacent moored water craft and, when we were heading directly for the bow of a giant cruiser, out came the gang plank which served as the perfect oar!

Being closer to the water, it was most pleasant to listen to the gentle lapping against the side of the boat, while breathing in the warm air from the breeze that blew around us.

The mute captain displayed a myriad of coloured beads, wooden carved animals and bendy wooden crocodiles which he carefully placed on the floor of the boat. Unfortunately he didn't sell much, as everyone had already bought handfuls of necklaces on the earlier motor boat.

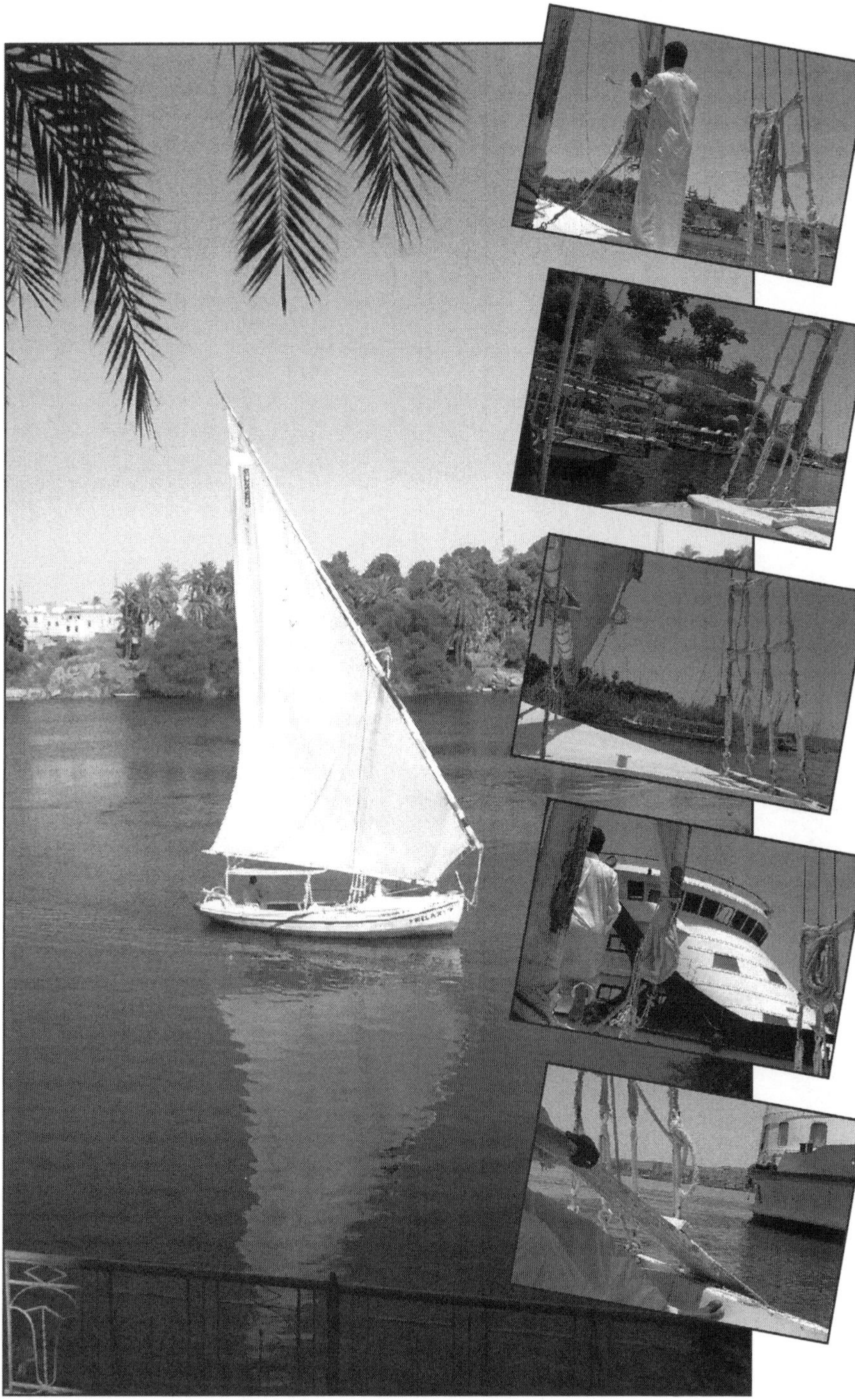

The felucca pulled up alongside the river-side door of our ship and we were each passed from crew hand to crew hand and climbed on a chair to get back on board! Quite charming!

As the call to prayer sounded out from the minarets surrounding the ship, we were advised not to go into Aswan in the afternoon as there was a planned demonstration after Friday prayers. Things were outwardly calm but obviously not finally settled. Any reference to Mubarak's name had been removed (even from streets and buildings) and the people were still unsettled.

Back in time for lunch.

A quick 'rest' after lunch, and we took the optional 'Nile Adventure' – and what an adventure it turned out to be!

Lunch Menu

Spinach slice – yum!
Cucumber and coleslaw salads
Chicken Chasseur
Chips
(yes, chips – you could see people's eyes lighting up!)
Fresh fish
Cakes, pastries and fresh fruit

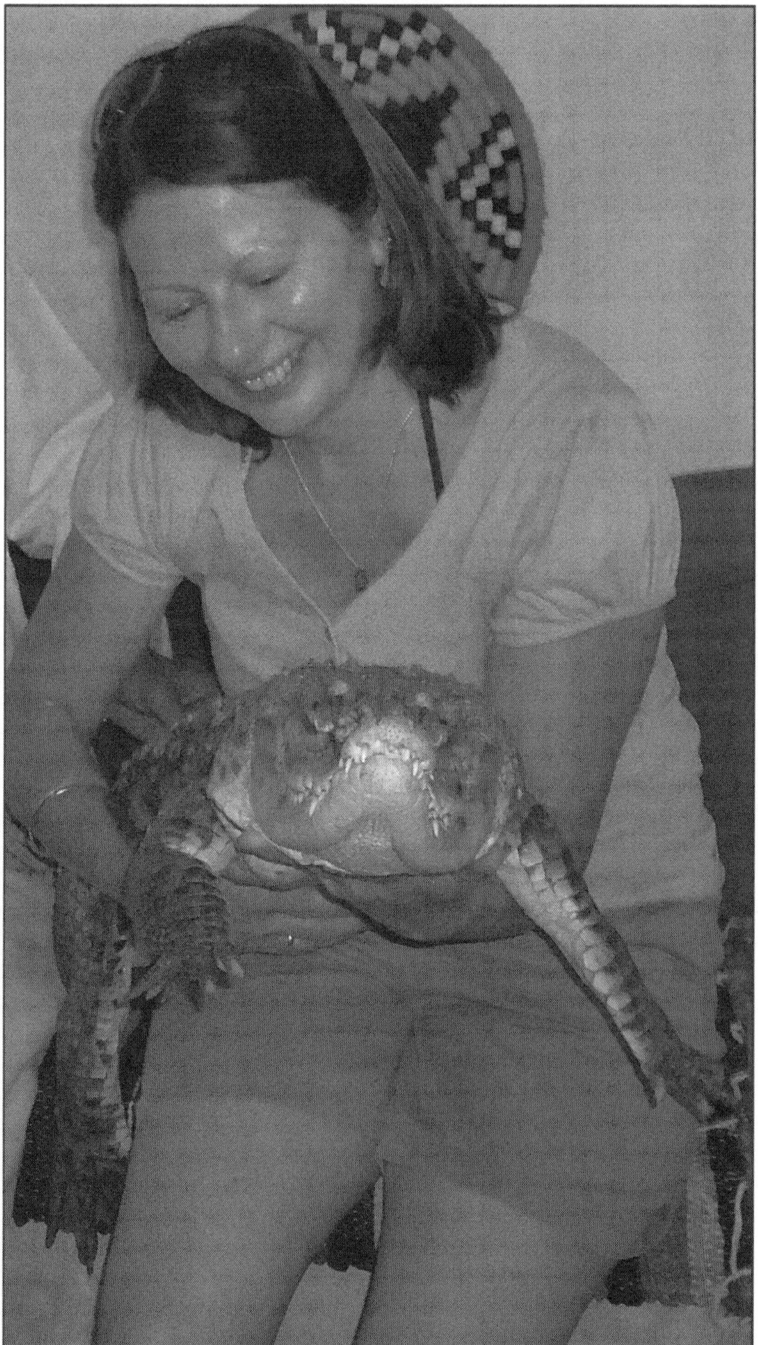

Nile Adventure

"Pay no money, give no tips, everything is already covered," we were told by Akil. OK!

A motor boat had moored next but one to our ship, so a 2 minute walk with not a street seller in sight and we were boarding the little boat, captained by Husani and his son, which took us across the Nile to Kitchener Island where we enjoyed a 40 minute visit to this little piece of botanical sanctuary, right in the middle of the river. There were exotic palms and innumerable interesting species I'd never seen before, some still in flower. There were tweets and squeaks from the native wildlife (not the electronic kind), birds flew from tree to tree and cats scavenged for scraps left by picnickers. There's a small museum on the site and a covered café area. Street sellers? Yes, but not that many and not too aggressive.

A half-hour upstream boat ride followed – beautifully relaxing, wafting us with a cooler breeze as we went along. It felt like the engine struggled to pass the swirling waters around the Cataracts, and the pace gave us a chance to take a photo of the Cataract Hotel where a certain famous author wrote her well-known murder mystery*.

Little boys on hand-made rafts paddled out to the motor boat, hanging on the side and singing 'She'll be Coming Round the Mountain When She Comes' and 'Frère Jacques' for coins. They were funny! I can't imagine they understood what they were singing, but they made us smile, and they made a few bob in the process!

Reaching a bend in the river where the water was clean, we pulled up and got off the little boat to feel the hot desert sand between our toes and to paddle in the surprisingly cold water of the Nile. Some brave souls even swam in it!

We decided to risk the camel ride from there to the Nubian village for LE70 each, paid to Akil – no bartering, no hassle. Great fun! Getting up and down on those animals is something of an achievement, as is hanging on without having your thumb muscles ripped out! My camel, Marr by name, had his rump nipped by the impatient animal following him and

*The Cataract Hotel where Agatha Christie wrote *Death on the Nile*

– yikes – he bolted (hence the ripped thumb muscles). If you do this, always hold on to the top of the knobbly bit on the saddle, not around the side of it – Lawrence of Arabia-like, I was not! The poor girl riding the offending camel was apoplectic with fear, having visions of herself and her ride careering sideways down the steep slope into the flowing waters below.

We arrived at the village with the locals hosing down the dusty road. The houses were all colourfully decorated with paintings of flowers and crocodiles – it was the crocodiles we had come to see. The road was lined with busy, dusty stalls selling the by-now familiar scarves, scarabs, cat figurines, Egyptian dresses and we found an artist making sand pictures in bottles for £2-3 each. There was very little hassle here with the sellers – maybe they were well-paid by the tour companies to be more relaxed. The hairy part was getting out the way when the real Lawrences hurtled towards us on their own speedy, much bigger and frankly cleaner-looking camels, complete with velvet drapes with bobbly, bouncing tassels.

The village house we were 'invited' to was mostly roof-less, except for a rattan cover. Most of the floor was sand which they cleaned by raking. In the middle of the main room were two large concrete crocodile pens, covered with metal grills. The large pen contained Daddy Croc – fierce and scary. In the smaller pen were two babies, each one about a metre long. The 'chief' of the house carefully lifted one of the babies and invited each of us to sit beside him and hold the crocodile. Melody was the first one there – she was braver than any of us! When it came to my turn, I found it lovely to the touch – cool and rather like a football that was only two thirds blown up.

The crocodiles these days are kept purely for tourist entertainment. Financially, this obviously pays off for the owners. As the crocodiles showed no sign of wanting to eat us, we surmised they were well-fed and looked after.

Our hosts invited us to look around their house. They were fiercely proud of it. On the top floor was a flat roof which could be used as an outdoor space in cooler temperatures. They had a little kitchen with a stove; in another room there was a washing machine with the most wonderful blue and yellow flowery zip-up cover (including a round fitted bit for the door) and in the bedroom, la pièce de résistance – a giant flatscreen TV. To complete the menagerie, there was a seriously scary, old stuffed fox guarding a brood of live hens under the stairs and a cooler cabinet full of Coke in the hall.

We wandered back to the awaiting motor boat, taking care to avoid the hurtling camels and riders, and bought bottles with sand pictures in on the way.

Throughout all this trip, we had left all our 'valuable' belongings on the motor boat. Husani and his son had diligently watched over the boat and everything was there, exactly as we had left it. Later that evening, Akil approached us with Ellen's sunglasses. She'd left them on the boat and the captain had taken the trouble to return them to our ship. Now that did deserve a baqsheesh!

The half-hour return trip was made even more enchanting for the youngsters (and some oldies) who climbed up on to the roof of the speeding boat. With the exhilarating wind in their hair, there was a great view of the golden pink sky as the sun set beyond the horizon.

There was just time for quick shower (or a pool dip for some younger members) before dinner.

That evening, it was showtime! A special Nubian show exploded in a cacophony of native instruments and singing. The traditionally-dressed dancers wearing long, billowing robes, whirled and twirled and cajoled us poor spectators into joining in. Suffice to say, we all looked extremely silly trying to copy their actions but had great fun. After the dancing, the special Nubian panto horse put in an appearance, nudging all the men and 'kissing' all the pretty young women and girls.

Back in our cabin, the towel sculptors had excelled themselves; a pair of sunbathers made of towels and bolster cushions awaited us, together with a mosquito that Ellen finally managed to squish with a book. (Did I mention to take fly spray?)

Philae Temple

The inevitably-rising water levels (due to the lower dam in Aswan which was erected in 1902 by the British) and barrages during annual inundations, meant the Island of Philae (amongst others) and its monuments, lay half-submerged. During the UNESCO rescue operations of the Nubian monuments in the 1960s, the temple complex of Philae was moved, piece by piece, and reassembled on the island of Agilkai, 550 metres away.

The earliest building on the island of Philae was a small temple dedicated to Isis, built by Napktnebef Kheperkare (Nectanebo I) in about 370 BC. This was later expanded to become the Great Temple of Isis by a number of rulers, most notably Ptolemy II Philadelphius (285-246 BC) and Diocletian (284-305 AD).

Philae was one of the last outposts of Egyptian religion, surviving two centuries after the Roman Empire converted to Christianity. The sacred island attracted many Greek and Roman pilgrims, who came to pray for healing from the mysterious Egyptian goddess, Isis. Even after their defeat by Emperor Marcian in 451 AD, Nubian priests were permitted to make offerings to Isis on Philae.

The temples were finally closed in 535 AD by order of Byzantine Emperor Justinian. Some of the chambers were converted for Christian worship and a Coptic community (native Egyptian Christians) lived on the island until the coming of Islam.

The largest and most important temple on Philae is the Great Temple of Isis. The west colonnade boasts a subterranean staircase leading down to a small 'Nilometer', which was used to measure the height of the Nile each year. The higher the Nile, the higher the taxes, as it meant the farmers could grow more crops.

West of the forecourt, just behind the First Pylon, is the Birth House (Mammisi). This was dedicated to Hathor-Isis in honour of the birth of her son, Horus and was where the king conducted rituals securing his legitimate decendancy from Horus.

Behind the Second Pylon is the Temple of Isis itself, which consists of a court, a vestibule, several antechambers and the inner sanctum where the sacred image of Isis was kept.

About 50m east of the Temple of Isis is the little Temple of Hathor, built by Philometor and Euergetes II in honour of Hathor-Aphrodite.

Entrance price:
adults LE50, children LE25

The Rosetta Stone

The Rosetta Stone is, as the name suggests, a stone, with writing on it in two languages (Egyptian and Greek), using three scripts (hieroglyphic, demotic and Greek).

The first is hieroglyphic which was the script used for important or religious documents. The second is demotic, the common script of Egypt. The third is Greek which was the language of the rulers of Egypt at the time. Three scripts were used so that the priests, government officials and rulers of Egypt could all read what it said.

The inscription is a decree passed by a council of priests. It is one of a series that affirms the royal cult of the 13 year old Ptolemy V on the first anniversary of his coronation.

The Rosetta Stone was carved in 196 BC and found in 1799 by French soldiers who were rebuilding a fort in a small village in the Delta called Rosetta, hence the name.

After many years of studying the Rosetta Stone and other examples of ancient Egyptian writing, Jean-François Champollion, who could read both Greek and Coptic, deciphered the hieroglyphs in 1822 in Paris.

It has been on public display at the British Museum since 1802.

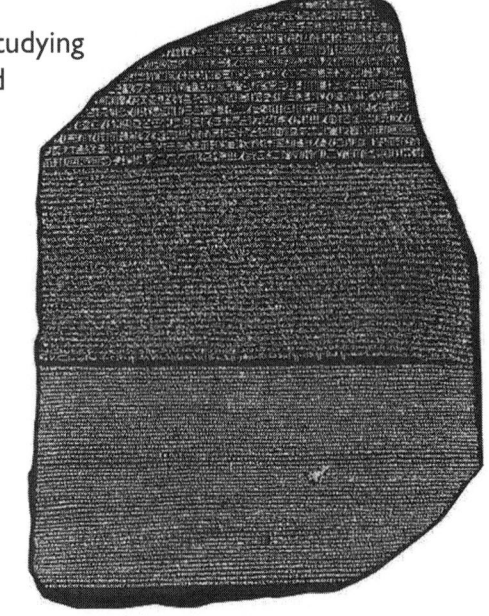

Dinner Menu

Choice of salad
Soup
Roast chicken
Baked spinach
Beef chunks
Calamari
Fresh fruit and chocolate sponge

ندى و نور لملابس الأطفال

Saturday 9th July

Aswan
Optional visit to Abu Simbel Temple by coach
Cruise and overnight in Edfu
Evening on board Egyptian party

The Saturday morning was at leisure for most of us. Seven brave souls left at 4am to take in the wonders of Abu Simbel – a three-and-a-half hour coach ride (with bathroom!) each way, to return at around 1pm.

Such a journey, we wisely considered, was way beyond the tolerance of our youngest. Had our party consisted of adults alone, we would indeed have made it but by now, we were already struggling with her tiredness and impatience to arrive at the hotel 'with 30 water slides' we'd promised for later on in the week.

Our family outing, we decided, would be a foray into the old traditional souk in Aswan. To get off our ship, we had to walk through two others that were docked in front of us for renovation. Luckily the ships are built so all the doors line up! As we walked along the street the car horns beeped constantly, the horses' hooves clattered on the road and people were shouting to each other. Plan A was to head for the MacDonald's we'd spotted from the motor boat, buy a drink and break a LE50 note. Immediately we left the ship, an Egyptian guy dressed in long traditional robes tried to persuade us on to a caleche ride, then promptly proceeded to try and pick Ken's pocket! A second man in a darker robe rushed up beside us apologising, lamented his fellow countryman's misdeeds, and insisted on guiding us to where we wanted to go. Under no circumstances was he taking 'no' for an answer!

Changing the LE50 in MacDo was easier said than done. Permission from the manager was necessary for this little transaction! Opposite MacDo is a bank with a cash machine, the post office and police station, in case you need it.

Our newly-acquired guide waited patiently outside, keeping his eyes peeled for a better prospect. Finding none, he latched himself onto us the minute we emerged into the heat of the morning. He 'guided' us into a shop at the entrance to the souk and promised, "No hassle." He was right, it was like an oasis. Ellen bought a silver chain and we chose a perfume bottle for our neighbour who was feeding our cat, and a new fan for Melody to keep herself cool. The owner claimed to have a sister living in East Anglia and had a tea-towel to prove it! He even had an ASDA* bag pinned to the wall and claimed his prices were ASDA price!

Out in the market again, guess who? Yes, you got it. We paid him off and he disappeared only to be replaced by another 'guide' wearing a light brown gown, with matching brown front tooth. Incredibly, he knew which ship we were on – he must have been watching us since the time we left. Now I was worried!

10am is early for markets by Egyptian standards. The stall owners were nosily winding up their shutters (those who had them) and there were people milling around, hosing down the dusty strip. There were spice stalls with their rich aromas and beautifully coloured baskets full of cumin, hibiscus leaves and many other exotic spices, mingling with the diesel smell from the odd motor bike weaving in between the shoppers. Alabaster statues of the Egyptian gods, black basalt figurines, delicate glass perfume bottles, brightly coloured clothes and towels waving around in the wind, coolers full of Coke and Tango. The bakers displayed their flat breads and pastries in front of old buildings covered with peeling paint – it was a melange of heat, delicious scents and a mild, underlying tension. We were the only western tourists in the place!

Suddenly another European family appeared in front of us! We hung back hoping they would get all the attention but they very inconsiderately disappeared into a shop. Aghh!

Most of the stall holders were friendly and invited us to look around. We bought black cat statues and little pyramids made of basalt and blue china scarabs for the girls, all for small change. The souvenirs were easy to buy. It was the Ice Tea that caused the furore!

Ice tea is our girls' favourite drink. In Switzerland it is one of the most popular soft drinks you can get, but in Egypt it is a pretty rare commodity. Mr Brown Tooth finally cottoned on to our search and suddenly rushed off in front, returning a minute later with a tin of the illusive thirst quencher – OK, maybe he would deserve a tip after all! We asked for two more tins and suddenly we were surrounded by his 'gang' members. Two more guys pounced on us. "Sit in the shade," said one, who beckoned us to a make-shift tent. A small, bright pink stool was pulled out. "Sit, sit." Melody sat. A woman appeared in full black headdress and gown eagerly clutching three tins of... Tonic Water! A jabber of shouting in Arabic ensued. The Head Honcho muscled in and tried to steal our LE50 note. Maybe he succeeded – with his deft hand movements, I couldn't be sure.

*ASDA is a great, value-for-money supermarket in the UK

My endeavour to remain calm dissolved and at this point, I lost the plot. "Give me back our money!" I shouted.

By now, Mr Brown Tooth had decided there was no chance of a tip and had surreptitiously disappeared, sneaking off down a side street.

We escaped as fast as we could. Luckily they did not follow. We'd slightly lost our bearings in our Quest for the Great Ice Tea, however, a left turn and across the road brought us back onto the more respectable main street running alongside the river.

A quick McFlurry in the icy cool sanctuary of MacDo, and a sneaky descent to the little tow path on the river bank where the ships dock, took us safely back to the Champollion without further ado.

We were a little late leaving Aswan to head back for Luxor as the Abu Simbel party were slightly delayed. They were exhausted but exhilarated at the wonderful sights they had seen. Photography being forbidden, Colin was annoyed to discover he'd left the post cards he'd bought on the tour bus. He was looking forward to a quiet afternoon nap!

After lunch, we spent the afternoon lazing on the sun deck, mostly hiding from the heat and some of the other passengers, in the pool which had an ingenious shallow area, about 20cm deep around a deeper pool, which you could quite nicely lie in and keep cool.

Akil had an arrangement with a jeweller in Luxor. That afternoon, the girls chose a silver bracelet and a necklace with their names in ancient Egyptian letters spelled out inside a 'cartouche'. They would be specially made for them in the workshop and delivered to us when we reached Luxor.

In these quiet times for Egypt tourist-wise, we were told that in high season (Winter), the cruise ships docked at Aswan were five deep and that every one was fully booked. Out of 300 ships, 14 were running whilst we were there. We were the third ship in our dock. Many others were only two or one ship deep – the ships behind us were not fully booked. They weren't in service at all – they were in for 'renovation'. This was a bonus for us in some ways. The temples we visited were bereft of visitors and the river was quiet.

Aswan Market

If you are completely fazed by aggressive hassle, this is not a place for you. If however, you want to experience the souk atmosphere, have left anything you want to keep back on the ship and are prepared to get stuck in to a good barter, this is an interesting experience, go for it. Aswan is one of the larger cities and is bound to be rougher and tougher than the little side streets running up to the temples away from the city.

Dress appropriately. Try to blend in with the locals.

Have small change. LE50 notes are too big to get changed easily, even in big name shops. Keep money, phones and other valuables in zipped up pockets.

Tip

I found it useful to divide my notes up so I had LE10 in one pocket and LE20 in another, etc. That way I could get out the exact money I needed without showing what else I had, also the less scrupulous traders wouldn't be tempted to try and snatch my LE50 notes and swap them for 50 Piaster notes which look very similar! It's very distracting when the price you are haggling over constantly changes – up and down! Don't get your money out until you have agreed. Even then, in some cases, they will try and get you to pay more.

Don't get into a conversation with anyone unless you really do want them to act as a guide and are prepared to pay a trip.

Don't be afraid of going into the little shops – they are mostly comparatively hassle-free zones.

Haggling – generally we got items for just over half the starting price. If you are prepared to haggle further you may get things cheaper. We considered it wasn't worth it for what was really the equivalent of a few pence. After all, these people do have to earn their living.

For the fainter-hearted, there's a lot to be said for buying souvenirs on organised trips where the locals seem to have been paid by the tour companies not to hassle you. The wares are more or less the same wherever you go.

The cartouche

A cartouche is an oblong, or oval, surrounded by a magical rope which was drawn to protect the ancient Egyptian hieroglyphics that spelt out the name of a king or queen.

The survival of the name was imperative to the ancient Egyptians as they believed that the person would live for as long as the name was spoken and great efforts were made to protect it. Names of despised pharaohs, for example, Akhenaten, were obliterated from monuments and erased from documents to destroy all memory of him.

Cartouches were first used at the beginning of the 4th Dynasty under Pharaoh Sneferu. Before then, the names of kings and gods were written in rectangular frames. The cartouche was known in ancient Egypt as the shenu (derived from the Egyptian word 'sheni', meaning to encircle). Occasionally the name of the pharaoh can be seen together with the name of a god or goddess in a cartouche. In particular, Osiris and Isis in temple hieroglyphic inscriptions. In the tomb of the Pharaoh Tuthmosis III in the Valley of the Kings, the entire burial chamber, as well as the sarcophagus, was constructed in the form of a cartouche. Seen as a powerful, protective symbol, the form of the cartouche was often used in ancient Egyptian jewellery.

The word 'cartouche' was first applied to the symbol by the French soldiers who were part of the 1798 military campaign led by Napoleon Bonaparte into Egypt. They knew that Bony had given orders for the ancient Egyptian antiquities to be transferred to Paris and that the French scholars who accompanied the soldiers were interested in Egyptian history. The frequently-appearing symbol in the ancient Egyptian hieroglyphs resembled a gun cartridge, or bullets – the phrase 'gun cartridge' is 'cartouche' in French.

Saturday night is Egyptian party night! Everyone was in good spirits and some of our fellow passengers had dressed the part superbly – long robes, beautifully embellished with golden embroidery, besplendent in sequins and glass beads. The head dresses were spectacular, although somewhat unbearably hot in the struggling air con system.

We ate a wonderful salad of beans, pulses, chopped leaves, vegetables and even liver slivers! This was followed by a hot self-service buffet and our very own Chinese Chef, whisking up stir-fry vegetables in front of us.

After dinner a photographer in a long, shiny black robe coerced the party goers into Egyptian poses on the ornate staircase. It was all good fun and the atmosphere was jovial – but with extremely tired children and an early start the next day, we decided to give the party a miss.

The cabin was unusually warm so Ken went to ask if the air con could be stepped up a notch or two (knowing full well it couldn't). The attendant came in saying, "Engineer," which we knew, unfortunately, was just lip service, however, we'd made our point. The staff would have done something about it if they could. Frustratingly, the cabin on the floor above at the end of the corridor (occupied by those of Bedouin GPS fame) was purportedly too cold and the said occupants had got the blankets out! We consoled ourselves by admiring the boat and swan towel sculptures on a wavy sea and ordered in a bottle of wine, complete with ice bucket.

That night we decided to sleep with our heads at the other end of the bed. Anything to be nearer the air con outlet! Exhausted, I fell asleep without cleaning my teeth or taking my make up off – a shock-in-waiting for Sunday morning!

The ship docked overnight in Edfu.

Abu Simbel

Abu Simbel is an archaeological site comprising two massive rock temples in southern Egypt along the Nile about 290km south-west of Aswan. It was built by Ramses II, a 19th Dynasty pharaoh. He ruled for an extraordinary 67 years during the 13th Century BC.

The Great Temple of Ramses II is 35m long and 30m high. Flanking the entrance are four seated colossal figures, each a 20m high depiction of Ramses himself. Around the figures' knees are small carvings of some of his wives and children. It is aligned so the sun's rays travel through the mountain and illuminate Ramses' sanctuary twice a year — on October 22 and February 22.

Located 120 metres away is the Small Temple, a monument to his most beloved queen (out of his many wives), Nefertari. It is also dedicated to the ancient Egyptian goddess, Hathor. The Small Temple facade is about 28m long by 12m high. The entrance is marked by six colossal figures, each over 10m in height. There are four figures of Ramses himself and two of Queen Nefertari.

This temple marks only the second time in the history of ancient Egypt that a pharaoh dedicated a temple to one of his wives. It was also the first time that the statue of the wife, Nefertari in this case, was carved the same size as the image of the pharaoh himself. Usually, the wives' statues never measured higher than the pharaoh's knees.

Along with the six colossi stand smaller statues that represent Ramses' and Nefertari's children.

Construction of the temple complex started in approximately 1284 BC and lasted for around 20 years.

With the passing of time, the temples became covered in sand. By the 6th Century BC, the sand covered the statues of the main temple up to their knees. The temple was forgotten until 1813, when Swiss orientalist, J.L. Burckhardt found the top frieze of the main temple. Burckhardt shared his discovery with Italian explorer, Giovanni Belzoni, who travelled to the site but was unable to dig out an entry to the temple. Belzoni returned in 1817, this time succeeding in entering the complex.

In 1959 an international donations campaign to save the monuments of Nubia began: the southernmost relics of this ancient human civilization were under threat from the rising waters of the Nile that were about to result from the construction of the Aswan High Dam.

The salvage of the Abu Simbel temples began in 1964 and cost some USD $80 million. Between 1964 and 1968, the entire site was cut into large blocks, dismantled and then reassembled in a new location – 65m higher and 200m from the river.

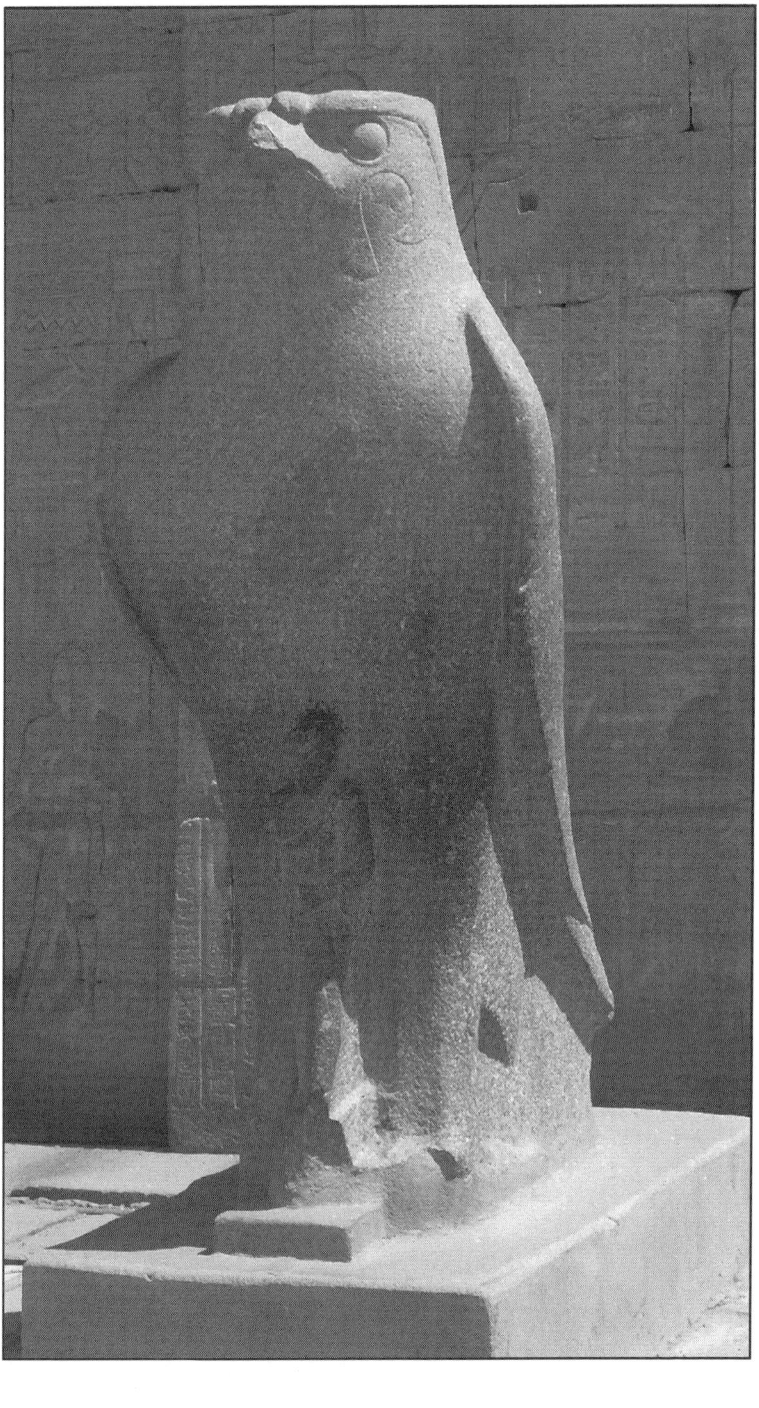

Sunday 10th July

Morning visit to Edfu Temple by horse-drawn carriage
Cruise and overnight in Luxor

Wake-up call: 8am. The girls were sound asleep and really didn't want to be woken up. Having repaired my teeth and face, we headed for the dining room and passed a stand displaying photos of the costumed party-goers from the night before, complete with snazzy Egyptian-style borders. It seems we weren't the only ones who wern't at the party. The budding Egyptians who had got all dressed up were most disappointed that it had been abruptly cancelled, apparently due to lack of interest – much to everyone's surprise! I imagined the queue at the ship shop's door that morning with angry revellers demanding refunds on all the costumes they'd bought only days or even hours before!

After breakfast we looked out of the window to see a row of caleches. Were we going to the temple by carriage? We were! This was great fun. On the journey, the caleches weaved about, vying for their place on the road alongside the vans beeping their horns, donkeys pulling carts, the motorbikes and the taxis, not to mention the pedestrians! Our caleche driver, Akins, was friendly and pointed out items of interest. At one point, our horse noticed an approaching incline and decided he had no intention whatsoever of climbing it. Akins cajoled him along, running in front of the horse, pulling his reigns and jumping back on with spritely agility once he'd got the reluctant animal going again. He let the girls take turns in 'driving' the caleche, telling them what good cart drivers they made and that they should do this for a living when they grew up – great! No further education fees to worry about for us, then!

We were mega-hassled running the gauntlet from the shady horse park to the temple entrance. By now we'd seen enough dresses, scarabs and beaded hats to last us for the next ten years, so the poor guys didn't stand a chance of selling anything, hungry to do so as they were. Small children were trying to sell bracelets. "One English pound, lady." Rude as I felt, in order to avoid engaging with the vendors, I adopted a strategy of keeping my mouth resolutely shut and my eyes fixed firmly on the ground. That worked!

The temple, although one of the best preserved by virtue of its having been buried in the sand, had peculiar smoke damage to the ceilings, apparently caused by fires lit by the latter Christian occupants. Restoration is currently impossible due to the fact that if the charring is removed, whatever treasures lie beneath would go with it. So, unrestored it remains until a satisfactory solution is found.

Many of the carvings have been defaced by Christians who lived there. You can see how high the sand was piled against the walls by the level at which the defacings have occurred.

As in many of the other places we visited, the temple came complete with 'Nileometer'. Here it consisted of a small passageway descending down a carved staircase next to one of the outer walls. At the bottom of the stairs – the Nile.

Driving back through the streets of Edfu was incredible. You will have to imagine the beep-beeps, the yells, the dust and the bumpy roads, the horses weaving around the taxis and cyclists, all on whichever side of the road they found a vacant slot, together with some fairly near misses.

We arrived back at the ship shaken and stirred and gave the driver a well-deserved tip. Another enterprising chap thrust the photo

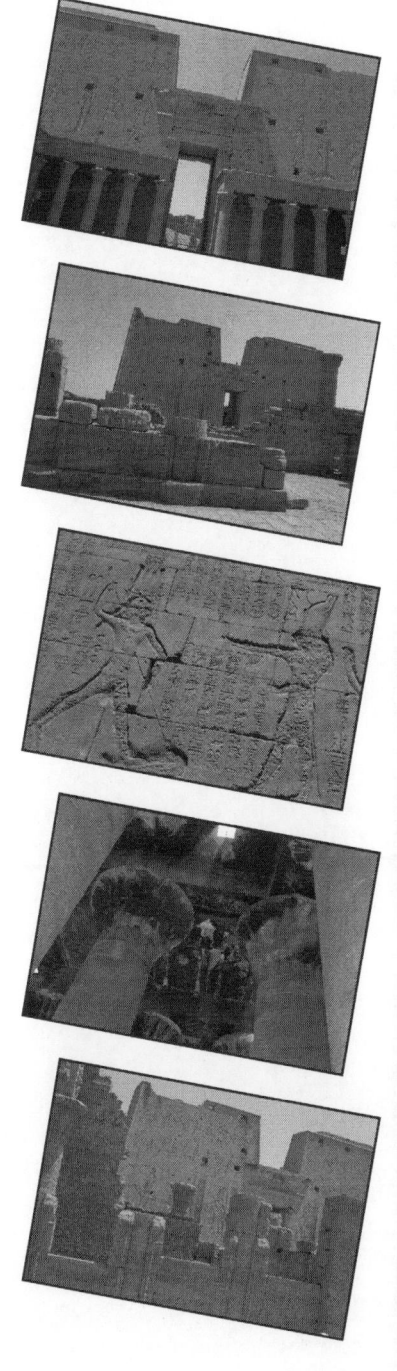

Lunch Menu

Pizza

Selection of salads

Breaded chicken

Chips

Green beans

Ice cream

Fresh fruit and chocolate sponge

he had taken of us climbing into the caleche under our noses. He'd had them printed in an Egyptian-themed folder whilst we'd been baking on our latest temple tour. You have to take your hat off to these people for trying to make a buck.

Welcoming us back on board were cold, wet towels and real lemonade. A quick dip before lunch was followed by an equally quick visit to the bridge to see the ship's captain piloting us back to Luxor.

Disappointingly there was no great wheel to steer by, just three PlayStation-style joysticks and a few electrical switches – some of which had sticky tape over them. There was a radar (and a TV) but the good captain, having sailed the Nile for some 30 years, had no need of such modern contraptions (except the TV, no doubt!) and knew exactly where to sail, which sandbank to avoid and how to get a 72m long by 14m wide ship into a 18m wide lock – no problem!

After a scrummy lunch, ice cream was ceremoniously carried in at head height (still in its economy-sized plastic container) on a silver serving dish, complete with lid, perched on a mountain of ice.

It was still half melted by the time we got to eat it, despite the valiant efforts of the kitchen staff. Melody managed to get two scoops! It was really delicious!

We left Edfu during lunch, heading for Luxor. Our outbound leg of this journey had been during the night, so we'd not seen these particular banks of the Nile, nor the Esna Lock which we passed through after lunch.

One of our fellow passengers informed us that going through the lock would be like Loch Ness. OK...

The first lock we reached was the old one, long since disused. As we approached, a couple of mad guys in a tiny boat way below us in the water were holding up scarves and towels. How on earth did they think we could buy their offerings from there? They managed to throw a couple of towels on to the bridge. Surely the crew wouldn't be interested in buying this stuff? It got thrown back – they kept trying! Transactions, it seemed, were to be made by throwing money inside empty plastic bottles to each other.

The sunshades we had been sitting under at the front of the ship had now been lowered to fit under the first lock barrier, which meant we had to retreat to the large shade canopy at the rear of the ship. It was a bit noisier there than our more usual position, with some of the louder guests opinioning this and that, and had a 'sound system' tinkling out a mixture of Egyptian rock, 80s classics and 'Tubular Bells'.

The hot wind was strong this afternoon – enough to make it too cold to get out of the pool!

Approaching the new lock there were more vendors throwing towels and table cloths on board. "Asda price!", again. "Best quality," and "What colour you want?" echoed on to the sun deck. Asda price it may have been, quality it was not. A cheeky passenger offered to sell the towels to the other guests for a 20% cut but failed, nevertheless, to convince anyone to buy them – not that he had any intention of really selling anything – it was all just for amusement. The goods were all thrown back. As the lock emptied, we dropped closer and closer to the vendors' level. The barter stepped up a level, but luckily the ship never got low enough for them to board us. Funnily enough, the vendors were not interested in our yellow and white striped, best quality Egyptian cotton, ship's deck towels we tried to sell *them*, even at 10 pounds each – all good fun.

The afternoon passed lazily by. The passengers had taken to waving madly at their compatriots on the occasional passing ship to see how many would wave back. Various other competitions were hotting up, too. Whose wife was worth the most camels? Well, actually, I was winning to date with an offer of 20 million – on the condition I threw in my daughter, too, though!

We would dock in Luxor that evening and stay there for three nights. A fellow guest asked what would happen now – somewhat disappointed that our seven day cruise didn't actually include seven days of cruising. She had a point but the Luxor excursions would not have been possible without the stay there.

our dock at Luxor

CHAMPOLLION I

Edfu Temple

The Temple of Horus in Edfu, also known as the Temple of Edfu, is considered the best-preserved cult temple in Egypt. This is partly because it was built later than most in the Ptolemaic era from 237 to 57 BC.

Despite its later date, it exactly reflects the traditional architecture of the pharaohs and so gives a good idea of how all the temples would once have looked. Edfu is built on a grand scale.

The falcon-headed Horus was originally the sky god, whose eyes were the sun and moon. He was later assimilated into the myth of Isis and Osiris as the divine couple's child. Raised by Isis and Hathor after Osiris' murder by his brother, Seth, Horus avenged his father's death in a great battle at Edfu. Seth was exiled and Horus took the throne with Osiris reigning through him from the underworld. Thus all pharaohs claimed to be the incarnation of Horus, the 'living king'.

In 332 BC, Alexander the Great conquered Egypt. After his death in 323, his successors ruled under the Ptolemaic Dynasty, the last dynasty of independent Egypt. The Ptolemies were Greeks but presented themselves to the Egyptians as native pharaohs and closely imitated the traditions and architecture of pharaonic Egypt.

The temple was built during this Ptolemaic era on top of an earlier temple to Horus, which was oriented east-west instead of the current north-south orientation, and was abandoned after the Roman Empire became Christian, paganism being outlawed in 391 AD.

It became almost totally buried in sand, with homes built over the top, until it was excavated by Auguste Mariette in the 1860s. The sand protected the monument over the years, hence its state of preservation.

At the back of the Court of Offerings, outside the Hypostyle Hall, are a pair of black granite Horus statues. One stands taller than a man and gives the perfect photo opportunity; the other lies legless on the ground.

A small doorway, decorated with reliefs of the sacred barques (barges) of Horus and Hathor, leads from the Festival Hall into the Hall of Offerings. During the New Year Festival, the image of Horus was carried up the ascending stairway to be revitalised by the sun, then carried back down the descending stairway.

This hall leads into the Sanctuary of Horus, the holiest part of the temple. The sanctuary centres on a black granite shrine that was dedicated by Nectanebo II, making it the oldest relic in the temple which once contained the gilded wooden cult image of Horus. Next to the shrine is an offering table and the ceremonial barque on which Horus was carried during festivals.

The passage in the west wall leads to a corridor with images of the triumph of Horus over Seth. Specifically, they depict a Mystery Play that was performed as part of a festival ritual, in which Seth appears as a hippopotamus lurking beneath his brother's boat. At the end of the play, the priests cut up and ate a hippo-shaped cake.

The provincial town of Edfu is located about halfway between Luxor (115km away) and Aswan (105km), and is 65km north of Kom Ombo.

Entrance price: adults LE50, children LE25

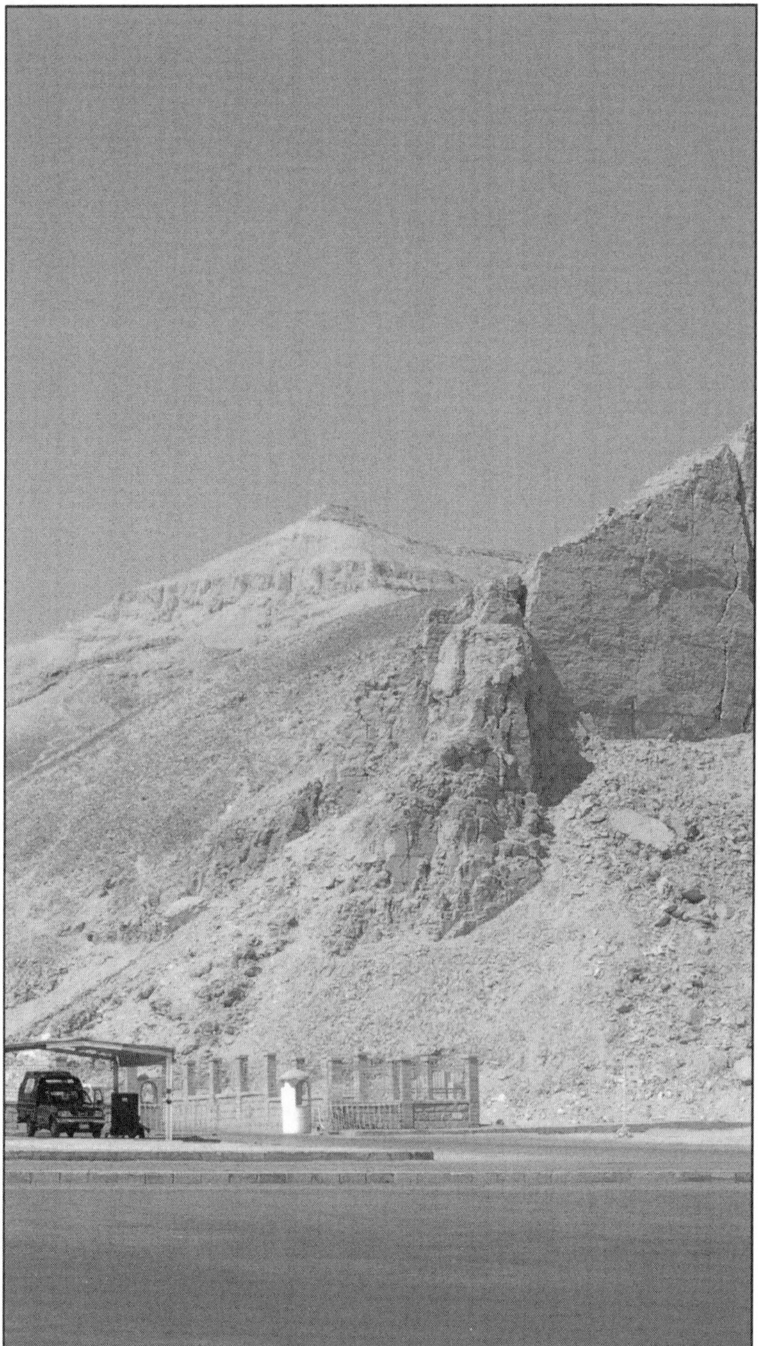

Monday 11th July

Morning West Bank visit to the Valley of the Kings,
Valley of the Queens, Habu Temple and Colossi of Memnon
Optional evening sound and light show in Luxor
Overnight in Luxor

If it's Monday, it must be Valley of the Kings day. 5am wake-up call! We lethargically ate the usual breakfast and were on board the coach by 6.15am. The coach ride took us over the Falcon Bridge from the East to the West Bank – a manic ride worthy of a theme park attraction with mega-bouncy coach suspension! On the way, the by-now familiar donkey-drawn carts, pedestrians and taxis passed noisily by.

The West Bank is unique. On one side of the road to the Valley of the Kings, many of the houses have been turned into alabaster 'factories' and are cheerfully painted on the outside. The contrast with the opposite side of the road is stark. The former residents had been moved out a few years ago and the empty villages are gradually being demolished to excavate as yet undiscovered tombs below.

Boarding the little train which would save us the long walk to the entrance (complete with armed guard), we were the first group of the day to arrive at the Valley of the Kings. The heat

Valleys of the Kings and Queens

No cameras are allowed in. You can buy postcards.

Your entrance ticket at LE80 will give you access to three tombs of your choice. At the main entrance there's a list of all the particular tombs open that day. If you want to visit King Tut's tomb, it will cost you an extra LE100 (we were advised against this by more than one person as it is the smallest tomb in the valley and only has two painted walls. All the contents are distributed amongst various museums, mainly Cairo). A mini-train ride, complete with armed guard, saved us the hot walk to the tomb entrances. The tombs have long corridors, just big enough to get a sarcophagus through, leading downwards into the earth. The walls and ceilings are mostly richly decorated and it is fascinating to try and make out the stories depicted. There are carvings of all the gods, as well as paintings of limbless, headless or horizontal figures representing the slaves or the enemies of the king and huge images of the king hacking and slashing his enemies – all designed to frighten off potential tomb raiders. Other images show the king's life and suitable icons to aid his passing into the next world. It's stunning to see these figures in all their colourful glory.

Tip

If you want to visit a further three tombs, wander back to the entrance and buy yourself another ticket. At LE80, it has to be worth it.

We were warned that in high season, it could mean a half-hour wait to get in.

was already building and the omnipresent street vendors were hovering, waiting to ply their wears on us. We'd be warned not to buy any statues that were being displayed on newspaper (and we saw plenty) – this is because the paint would rub off immediately when you touch it. Akil sat us all down on benches under a sunshade, complete with fan, to explain the history of this mystical burial site. One by one, the street sellers closed in on us, only to be scolded away like dogs by our guide when they got too close.

Tour guides are not allowed in the tombs. A sensible rule, given their narrowness. Ticket punchers do not consider themselves as guides, however, and each one followed us from the entrance of his particular tomb, pointing out Horus, a crocodile or a three headed snake. They would even lend you a torch (quite unnecessary), all for a baqsheesh on the way out, of course! "Thank you, Madame!"

After our visit to the tomb of Ramses IV, our two other chosen tombs were Ramses VI and Ramses IX. The third was a good deal larger than the first two and interestingly, had to take a right turn when the original excavators met an existing tomb, forcing them to make a slight detour.

Adopting my 'rude' stance and ignoring the vendors completely, we wandered up a little path and discovered tomb number KV8 of Merenptah.

Its entrance was accessed by climbing a steep set of iron stairs. Sadly it was closed which was a real shame as we would have loved to have seen inside that one – what an ace place to hide the entrance! Thanks to a tip to the armed guard who sat by the stairs, we discovered the way in – around a rock and down a few more stairs. Luckily the guard was happy to be of help and declined shooting us on sight!

Each tomb is unique, telling its own story. This is an amazing place with an eerie, evocative atmosphere.

Indiana Jones had to be there at sunrise, somewhere!

We all boarded the little train for a breezy ride back to the main entrance. Some of the street vendors hopped on the train with us, hopeful of a last minute sale – no luck; however, when Colin's hat blew off in the wind, an enterprising vendor ran after it and charged him £1 to get it back – well, cheaper than a new hat, I suppose!

There are no mummies in the tombs. Legend has it that one particular family removed all the mummies and hid them in the nearby mountains, gradually selling off the riches and jewellery until the Antiquities Authorities caught wind of it. The surviving mummies were taken to a museum to try and sort out who was who.

The street vendors are maniacal. They sell books, which actually looked very interesting but I couldn't knock the guy down far enough to feel I'd got a bargain – which I thoroughly regret now, 'alabaster' figurines which were completely fake and broke easily and the famous figures which lose their paint on contact with human skin.

There's a café there. Expect to pay £5 for a can of Coke. We paid the £5 and were glad of the respite from the heat and the sellers, who were not allowed 'inside' – it's actually just a covered area.

As no cameras are allowed in the Valley of the Kings or the Valley of the Queens, we also left our mobile phones on the bus. Apparently if you are caught using them to take photos, they can be confiscated. This, as it turned out, was a mistake, as we were watch-less and had no idea what the time was!

There are currently just over 60 excavated tombs in the Valley of the Kings and many remain, still to be excavated. The tombs are numbered chronologically in the order in which they were found. Don't confuse the tomb of Ramses IX, which is number 6 with Ramses XI which is tomb number 4!

The colours in the tombs are fading. The moisture levels, I'm told, are attacking these stunning ancient works. Without air conditioning systems installed in the tombs, their brilliance cannot last and there are already signs of deterioration.

The Valley of the Kings was much 'cleaner' than I had expected, with proper roads and sun shelters, benches, maps and well-marked entrances – not the dusty desert archaeological dig site I'd had in mind. Shame!

Valley of the Kings

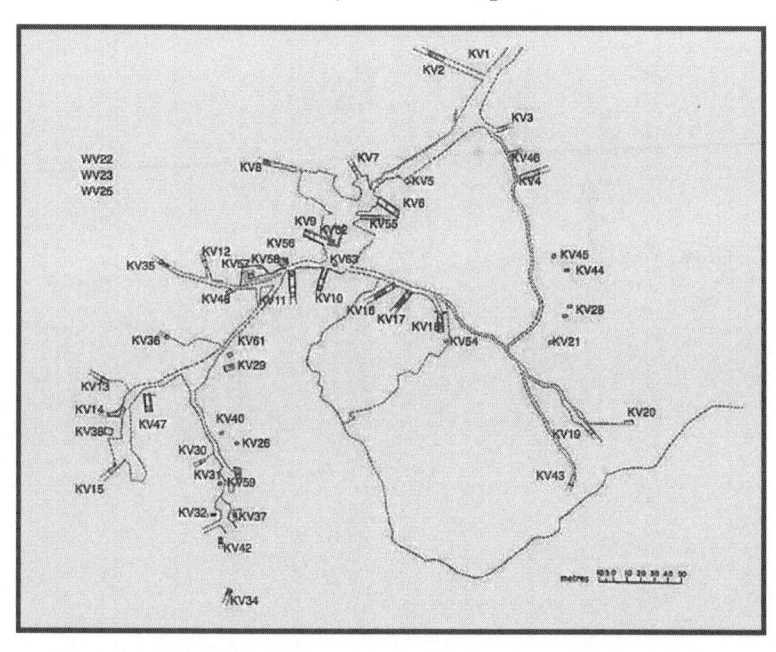

Tombs of the East Valley

KV1	Tomb of Ramses VII
KV2	Tomb of Ramses IV
KV3	Tomb of an unnamed son of Ramses III
KV4	Tomb of Ramses XI
KV5	Tomb of some of the sons of Ramses II With 120 known rooms and excavation work still underway, it is the largest tomb in the valley
KV6	Tomb of Ramses IX
KV7	Tomb of Ramses II
KV8	Tomb of Merenptah
KV9	Tomb of Ramses V and Ramses VI, also known as the Tomb of Memnon or La Tombe de la Métempsychose
KV10	Tomb of Amenmesse
KV11	Tomb of Ramses III (also known as Bruce's Tomb, the Harper's Tomb)
KV12	Occupant unknown; possibly used as a family tomb
KV13	Tomb of Bay and later Amenherkhepshef and Mentuherkhepshef
KV14	Tomb of Twosret, later reused by Setnakhte
KV15	Tomb of Seti II
KV16	Tomb of Ramses I
KV17	Tomb of Seti I and is also known as Belzoni's tomb, the tomb of Apis, or the tomb of Psammis, son of Necho
KV18	Tomb of Ramses X
KV19	Tomb of Mentuherkhepshef
KV20	Originally the tomb of Hatshepsut and Thutmose I
KV21	Unknown (as are KV 26-29)
KV30	Known as Lord Belmore's tomb; its original occupant remains unknown
KV31	Unknown
KV32	Tomb of Tia'a
KV33	Unknown
KV34	Tomb of Thutmose III
KV35	This tomb was originally the tomb of Amenhotep II. Over a dozen mummies, many of them royal, were relocated here
KV36	Tomb of the noble Maiherpri
KV37	Unknown
KV38	Tomb of Thutmose I
KV39	Possibly the tomb of Amenhotep I
KV40	Unknown
KV41	The original owner of this tomb is unclear, but it may have been Tetisheri
KV42	Tomb of Hatshepsut-Meryetre
KV43	Tomb of Thutmose I
KV44	Unknown
KV45	Tomb of the noble Userhet

KV46	Tomb of the nobles Yuya and Tjuyu, who were possibly the parents of Queen Tiy. Until the discovery of the tomb of Tutankhamun, this was the best preserved tomb to be found in the Valley
KV47	Tomb of Siptah
KV48	Tomb of the noble Amenemopet called Pairy
KV49	The original owner of this tomb is unknown, and it was possibly a store room
KV50	This tomb contains animal burials – which were possibly the pets of Amenhotep II, whose tomb is nearby
KV51 - KV53	These contained the burials of animals, and their precise location has been lost since their discovery
KV54	This was probably an embalming cache for the tomb of Tutankhamun
KV55	Tomb may be another mummy cache, and has the possible burials of several Amarna Period royals – Tiy and Smenkhkare/Akhenaten
KV56	The Gold Tomb; original owner unknown
KV57	Tomb of Horemheb
KV58	Chariot Tomb; original owner unknown
KV59	Unknown
KV60	Tomb of Sitre In
KV61	Apparently unused
KV62	The Tomb of King Tutankhamun
KVB - KVT	Non-burial pits, some of which may have been intended as tombs, others were probably funerary deposits

Tombs of the West Valley

The numbering of the West Valley tombs follows in sequence to that of the East Valley, and there are only four known burials/pits in the valley:

WV22	Tomb of Amenhotep III, one of the greatest rulers of the Egyptian New Kingdom. It has recently been investigated, but is not open to the public
WV23	Tomb of Ay and the only tomb that is open to the public in the West Valley
WV24	Unknown
WV25	This tomb may have been started as the Theban burial of Akhenaten, but it was never finished
WVA	This was a storage chamber for Amenhotep III's tomb which was located nearby

Deir el-Bahri (DB320)

This tomb contained an astounding mummy cache. It is located in the cliffs overlooking Hatshepsut's temple at Deir el-Bahri, was found to contain many of Egypt's most famous pharaohs. They were found in a great state of disorder, many placed in other people's coffins, and several are still unidentified.

Tricking the grave robbers

The original tombs had rectangular stones on top – making their location obvious to all and sundry. Desperate to prevent theft by grave robbers, it was decided that once the sarcophagus containing the dead king was safely inside the tomb, the entrance should be sealed and concealed.

To preserve the secret location of the tombs, the workers, who were reputedly well-treated, watered and fed, were blindfolded for the journeys to and from the tomb site. The eventual successful robbers were thought to have been workers' family members. You can imagine a father passing information to his son, "500 paces from up the well towards the rising sun, 360 paces descending down the stony road..." It couldn't have been that difficult to trace the locations. The tombs took many years to complete – no doubt the workers could find their way there with their eyes shut – literally!

After many failed attempts, Carter finally found the legendary King Tut's tomb. In a last ditch effort, he requested the workers' huts be moved so he could excavate beneath them and, lo and behold, guess what he found?

Rumour has it he actually found the tomb years before and was siphoning off the odd relic or two to sell to finance his digs.

The curse of the tombs

Would you want to be the worker who knocked the first hole in the tomb entrance thousands of years after it had been sealed? Absolutely not! If you breathed the air that exuded, you would be unlikely to survive. Not because of the fabled curses, but because you would have inhaled the poisons that were mixed with the Casein paint used to preserve the colours painted on the walls and ceilings.

The ancient paints were made using pigments derived from a variety of different methods and rocks. They were mixed with honey, egg and the afore-mentioned poison to ensure their endurance.

Red paint was created by using naturally oxidised iron and red ochre.

Green paint came from mixing oxides of copper and iron with silica and calcium, or from malachite.

White was made from chalk and gypsum.

Black could be made from carbon compounds like soot, ground charcoal or burnt animal bones.

Yellow came from natural ochres or oxides.

Blue was made by combining iron and copper oxides with silica and calcium.

The Valley of the Kings

The Valley of the Kings was created and used from approximately 1539 BC to 1075 BC. It contains over 60 tombs, starting with Thutmose I and ending with Ramses X. The official name of the site was The Great and Majestic Necropolis of the Millions of Years of the Pharaoh, Life, Strength, Health in the West of Thebes, or more usually, the Great Field.

The Valley of the Kings also had tombs for the favourite nobles and the wives and children of both the nobles and pharaohs. Around the time of Ramses I (c. 1300 BC) the Valley of the Queens was put into action, although some wives were still buried with their husbands.

The Valley of the Kings stands on the West Bank of the Nile, across from modern Luxor, under the peak of the pyramid-shaped mountain Al-Qurn. It is separated into the East and West Valleys, with most of the important tombs in the East Valley.

The West Valley has only one tomb open to the public: the tomb of Ay, Tutankhamun's successor. There are a number of other important burials there, including that of Amenhotep III, but these are still being excavated and are not publicly accessible.

The abbreviation KV ('King's Valley') is used to designate tombs located in the Valley of the Kings. Each tomb has been allocated a sequential KV number. Those in the Western Valley are known by the WV equivalent.

The tombs are numbered in the order of modern discovery, from Ramses VII (KV1) to Tutankhamun (KV62). Some of them have long since been open and KV5, the largest of the tombs, built for the sons of Ramses II, containing at least 67 burial chambers, has only recently been rediscovered. Graffiti on the walls of some of the tombs indicate that this was an attraction in ancient Greek and Roman times.

The most famous tomb is KV62, the Tomb of King Tutankhamun. The discovery of King Tut's tomb was made by Howard Carter on November 4, 1922, with clearance and conservation work continuing until 1932. Tutankhamun's tomb was the first royal tomb to be discovered that was still largely intact (although tomb robbers had entered it), and was the last major discovery in the valley. Despite the opulence of treasures found within, King Tutankhamun was actually a rather minor king and other burial chambers probably would have contained a bigger stash of treasure.

Some members of the archaeological teams led by Carter and others contracted lethal local viruses through food or animals (particularly insects), resulting in the infamous 'Curse of The Pharaohs' legend.

Entrance price to the Valley of the Kings: adults LE80, children LE40

Entrance price to the Valley of the Queens: adults LE35, children LE20

the Valley of the Queens

Next stop, Valley of the Queens – quite similar in outward appearance but smaller, less popular and with less shade, if that's possible! On the way we passed the Mortuary Temple of Queen Hatshepsut (Queen Hot Chicken Soup) without stopping to visit, which I found slightly disappointing. Although classed as being in the Valley of the Kings, and featuring in all the publicity photographs, it's not actually that close to the accessible tombs. It's an impressive monument built into the rock with an immense walk-way up to it with rows of statuesque columns and stark, flat terraces (well, that's what it looks like from a distance, anyway).

This is the temple where the dreadful massacre of 62 people (mostly tourists) by Islamic extremists that took place on 17 November 1997. Maybe that's why we didn't visit.

Arriving at the Valley of the Queens around 8am (although it felt like mid-afternoon!), the vendors' shops were not quite set up, but they followed us, merchandise in hand, none the less. A five minute meander took us past the toilet block – not bad facilities – a portacabin with running water. The attendant was kind enough to inform us he required a baqsheesh before allowing us in, handed us the allotted three sheets of loo roll each and promised to flush the toilets for us. I thought maybe this was a service too far, before we realised the handles were broken and there was no way we could do the job ourselves. Luckily he had some kind of control handle outside the cubicles. He had to settle for the £1 I gave him although he had clearly been expecting LE20. Expensive pee!

Again, one ticket, three tombs. Only three tombs were open that day. The 'most beautiful' tomb for the 'most beautiful' queen, Nefertari, was closed – costing a reputed €20 K to open it for a group visit.

The tombs were smaller but no less interesting or colourful than their respective counterparts across the valley. Besides queens, there are children and animals buried here.

The ticket punchers had their own little enterprises going – offering us dusty bits of cardboard to fan ourselves with. Baqsheesh, Madame, baqsheesh, please...?

In the middle of Akil's explanations, a second tour group arrived, whose guide decided to give her spiel right next to ours! Akil was not happy. Despite the heated Arabic exchange, the situation was not resolved. The place was empty – of all the tombs in all the valley, why did they have to stand right next to ours? I leave you to imagine the cacophony of rising voices, each competing to inform their respective listeners of the wonders of their surroundings. Don't forget the Arabic accents.

With so few visitors, it was a pleasure to wander around the tombs, admiring the beautiful paintings and carvings and trying to decipher the stories. The interiors were cool and shady. A welcome relief to searing sunshine outside.

Next on our itinerary was a visit to an alabaster factory. The handmade vases and objets d'art were quite stunning – lightweight and luminescent. There were even glow-in-the-dark figurines which were slime green in daylight –

fascinating! We were treated to a little demonstration on the pavement outside the shop with the resident artisan sitting cross-legged on a small stone on the floor, chiselling an egg-shaped lump of alabaster. He mimed the production processes using tools and pieces of alabaster in various states of preparation as they were described to us by our host, then we were led into the shop and offered the customary welcome drink.

The shop was stacked from floor to ceiling with black cats, green cats, brown sarcophagi, stone scarabs, lamp stands, vases of all colours, blue sphinxes, model pyramids, canubic jars with gods' heads on. You name it, in whatever size or colour you wanted, it was there, even bright black and gold replicas of King Tut's tomb – complete with desiccated mummy with detachable head inside! These were not souk prices, though, even after the bargaining, but still reasonable.

By now we were beginning to feel a bit templed-out. Melody was seriously struggling with tiredness. Choosing not to come into the alabaster shop, she wasn't thrilled to learn that we were going to visit yet another site. She should have been, though. This one was awesome!

these are some pictures from
'the other side of the road' to the
alabastor factories

Mortuary Temple of Queen Hot Chicken Soup

The Mortuary Temple of Hatshepsut is the focal point of the Deir el-Bahri (Northern Monastery) complex of mortuary temples and tombs located on the West Bank of the Nile, opposite the city of Luxor (ancient Thebes).

Hatshepsut was a rare female pharaoh. Her temple, known as Djeser-Djeseru (Splendor of Splendors), was designed and implemented by Senemut, the pharaoh's royal steward, for her posthumous worship.

Maatkare Hatshepsut, or Hatchepsut (late 16th Century BC - c. 1482 BC) was the fifth pharaoh of the 18th Dynasty. She is generally regarded by modern Egyptologists as one of the most successful pharaohs, ruling longer than any female ruler of an indigenous dynasty.

Hatshepsut was the daughter of Pharaoh Tuthmosis I and the wife of his successor Tuthmosis II, who died before she bore a son. Rather than step aside for the secondary wife who had borne him an heir, the plucky queen became co-regent of her stepson, the young Tuthmosis III. Soon she assumed absolute power.

To legitimise her powerful position, Hatshepsut had herself depicted with a pharaoh's kilt and beard. She was a prolific builder, commissioning hundreds of construction projects throughout both Upper and Lower Egypt. Under her reign, Egypt's trade networks began to be rebuilt, after their disruption during the Hyksos occupation of Egypt during the Second Intermediate Period.

She is believed to have ruled from 1503 to 1482 BC. Hatshepsut is regarded variously as the earliest known queen in history to have reigned in her own right, as the first known female to take the title Pharaoh, and the first 'great woman' in history, although all of these claims have been contested.

After Hatshepsut's death, Tuthmosis III became pharaoh. Perhaps fearing a challenge to his legitimacy as a successor, he immediately chiselled all images of Hatshepsut off temples, monuments and obelisks, consigning her remarkable reign to oblivion until its rediscovery by modern archaeologists.

A 100-foot causeway leads to the temple, which consists of three terraced courtyards covered in sculptural reliefs. Originally, sphinxes probably lined the path from the Nile to the base of the temple.

Next stop: Habu Temple.

In the past, Ramses III's name had been found in cartouches on temple walls far too numerous to have been constructed during his reign of around 60 years. Historians discovered he'd 'embellished' his predecessor's cartouches so they read III instead of II.

To avoid any such future plagiarism, his wall and column carvings were etched much deeper into the stone, avoiding all possibility of history repeating itself in the 'it's my temple' competitions of the time.

The rich colours were evident on many of the walls and the columns – quite breathtaking.

An attendant brandishing a pink, plastic broom beckoned us into a dark corner behind a barrier and pointed, "Look, look..." Ken being brave and curious followed. He beckoned to us girlies, too. Reluctantly we followed. Frankly, there was nothing to see, so either he thought we were interested in dark corners or he was thinking of attacking us. Not sure what an old codger with a pink, plastic broom could do, unless it was the equivalent of Hagrid's pink umbrella! Maybe he had hidden talents, so we beat a hasty retreat.

Outside was a really nice café with a most pleasant owner. All the prices were displayed and were fair and there were NO street vendors. This visit is a must! We sat in the café for a while before heading for the coach parked in a nearby stony car park, where little boys tried to sell us bracelets and trinkets.

A short drive and a quick photo stop at the Colossi of Memnon. Two giant figures which are very popular with the pigeons. Nothing to do with Memnon, apparently, they had made some kind of moaning sound in the past after their partial destruction by an earthquake. Reading up about it, I found it had originally been the entrance to the memorial temple of Pharaoh Amenhotep III – the remains of which have long since sunk into the ground.

With our visits over for the day, we rode the super bouncy coach back to the ship. In an interesting manoeuvre, the driver performed an impressive three point turn across the dual carriageway, on to the wrong side of the road, with two vehicles hurtling towards us. The trick, we decided, was to wait until the oncoming vehicles were pretty close before starting to pull across, then wait a bit longer until they were really close, then pull out as quickly as you could. This must be quite normal practice as the turn was completed with no major incident – not even a beep!

After lunch we hit the sun deck to recover from the morning's activities. A conversation with a native who lived in Sharm el Sheik had her explaining that once we got to Hurghada, we should go to a nearby town, 20 minutes up the road as, "It is much nicer and you wouldn't know you were in Egypt." Well, hey, why did we bother coming...?!

We spent the rest of the afternoon playing cards and watching bits of the video filmed by Camera Man. We knew it was him as he had 'camera man' embroidered on the back of his T-shirt! The TV had to be set up in the wrong aspect ratio, we all looked short and fat. (Note to self: never wear those shorts again and make sure you are at least a stone lighter for next time – I know my tummy is a little on the large side, but not that large!)

Ken said the same thing but by a stroke of 'luck' (not for Ken) Camera Man had caught us walking in the botanical gardens, *en famille*, Ken with his shirt unbuttoned. There was Melody, pointing to his tummy and covering it up quickly when she saw Camera Man coming! The shot was in the final cut and committed to DVD for all eternity.

We were beginning to find some fellow guests starting to complain about this and that. Some wanted tea and coffee to be free all day. Others wanted snacks to be available between meals (this could have been useful, assuming you could fit any more in). The fact that afternoon tea was only served during sailing days was cited as a bone of contention and the abundance of rice and eggs also seemed to be cause for concern. These were all fairly petty complaints made by those people intent on finding something to complain about – regardless of what it was.

This cruise was way beyond any of our expectations. We knew it would be 'hard work' to see all the wonderful temples, tombs and relics, which it was. It would have been nice to have had longer to explore these treasures (my little complaint). I understand the logic behind the early morning excursions to avoid the heat, however, the temperature difference wasn't really that great, so I was not convinced it would have made a huge difference to our comfort had the excursions been spread out a bit more over the day and some had taken place in the afternoons, rather than trying to cram everything in before lunch. My hours spent furiously peddling the exercise bike to get a bit fitter had certainly paid off. It made coping with the heat that much easier!

evidence of Christian occupation at Luxor

Habu Temple

Medinet Habu is the Arabic name for the Mortuary Temple of Ramses III, a huge, well-preserved complex.

The great pharaohs of ancient Egypt were buried in the Valley of the Kings but built great mortuary temples such as this one to honour their memory and to host the cult that connected them with the gods. Ramses III (1186-1155 BC) was buried in KV11 in the Valley and modelled his great mortuary temple on the Ramesseum of his ancestor Ramses II.

Ramses III was the second pharaoh of the 20th Dynasty and is considered the last great New Kingdom pharaoh to wield substantial authority over Egypt. During his long reign, Egypt was beset by foreign invaders (including the 'Sea Peoples' and the Libyans) and experienced the beginnings of the economic difficulties and internal strife which would eventually lead to the collapse of that Dynasty.

The site of Ramses III's mortuary temple was sacred long before his time and is still regarded as having magical powers by local farmers (fellaheen). During Ramses' lifetime, he often lived in the adjacent palace. Then and after his death, the statues of Amun, Mut and Khonsu visited every year during the Festival of the Valley; other deities resided at Medinet Habu permanently.

During the Libyan invasions of the late 20th Dynasty, Medinet Habu sheltered the entire population of Thebes. For centuries afterwards, it protected the Coptic town of Djeme, which was built inside its great walls. In Coptic times, a Christian church filled the Second Court of the temple.

Medinet Habu was first excavated sporadically between 1859 and 1899 by the Egyptian Antiquities Service, when the main temple was cleared, many Coptic buildings were removed and the site was made accessible to visitors. Since 1924, further excavations and conservation work has been led by Chicago University's Oriental Institute.

The best views of the entire temple complex, which is surrounded by partly-intact enclosing walls, can be had from the top of the mound near the south-east corner, or from a hot-air balloon ride. For a tip, a guard may be persuaded to unlock a stairway to the First Pylon, which provides excellent views.

The Mortuary Temple of Ramses III itself is made of sandstone. The First Pylon is about the same size as that of Luxor Temple, but has lost its cornice and one corner.

In Coptic times, the Second Court was used as a Christian church and the pillars were removed and the reliefs were plastered over with a thick layer of mud. The reliefs, now uncovered, still have their original colouring and depict the annual festivals of Min and Sokar. On the right side, a long text low on the wall records the events of Ramses' fifth year of rule.

Entrance price: adults LE30, children LE15

The Colossi of Memnon

Known to locals as el-Colossat, or es-Salamat, these are two massive stone statues of Pharaoh Amenhotep III. For 3,400 years they have sat in the Theban necropolis, across the Nile from the city of Luxor.

Originally, the Colossi stood guard at the entrance to Amenhotep's memorial temple, which was a massive cult centre built during the pharaoh's lifetime, where he was worshipped as a god-on-earth both before and after his departure from this world.

In its day, this temple complex was the largest and most opulent in Egypt, covering a total of 35ha. Later rivals such as Ramses II's Ramesseum or Ramses III's Medinet Habu were unable to match it in area; even the Temple of Karnak, as it stood in Amenhotep's time, was smaller.

With the exception of the Colossi, however, very little remains today of Amenhotep's temple. Standing on the edge of the Nile floodplain, successive annual floods gradually washed away the foundations and it was not unknown for later rulers to dismantle and re-use portions of their predecessors' monuments for building purposes.

It's thought that an earthquake in 27 BC shattered the northern colossus, causing it to collapse from the waist up. Following its disintegration, this statue was reputed to 'sing' every morning at dawn – a light moaning or whistling, probably caused by rising temperatures and the evaporation of dew inside the porous rock.

The legend of the 'Vocal Memnon' and the luck that hearing it was supposed to bring, travelled the length and breadth of the world. This attracted a constant stream of visitors, including several Roman Emperors, who came to marvel at the statues.

The mysterious vocalisations of the broken colossus ceased in 199 AD when Emperor Septimius Severus, in an attempt to curry favour with the oracle, reassembled the two shattered halves.

Memnon was a hero of the Trojan War, a King of Ethiopia who led his armies from Africa into Asia Minor to help defend the beleaguered city but was ultimately slain by Achilles. Whether associating the Colossi with his name was just a fanciful idea or wishful thinking on the part of the Greeks – they generally referred to the entire Theban Necropolis as the 'Memnonium' – the name has remained in common use for the past 2000 years.

The twin statues depict Amenhotep III (c. 14th Century BC) in a seated position, his hands resting on his knees and his gaze turned eastward toward the river and the rising sun.

Two shorter figures are carved into the front throne alongside his legs – his wife, Tiy and mother, Mutemwia. The side panels depict the Nile god, Hapy.

The statues are made from blocks of quartzite sandstone which was quarried at either Giza (near modern-day Cairo) or Gebel el-Silsileh (60km north of Aswan). Including the stone platforms on which they stand, they reach a towering 18 metres in height.

Entrance price: free

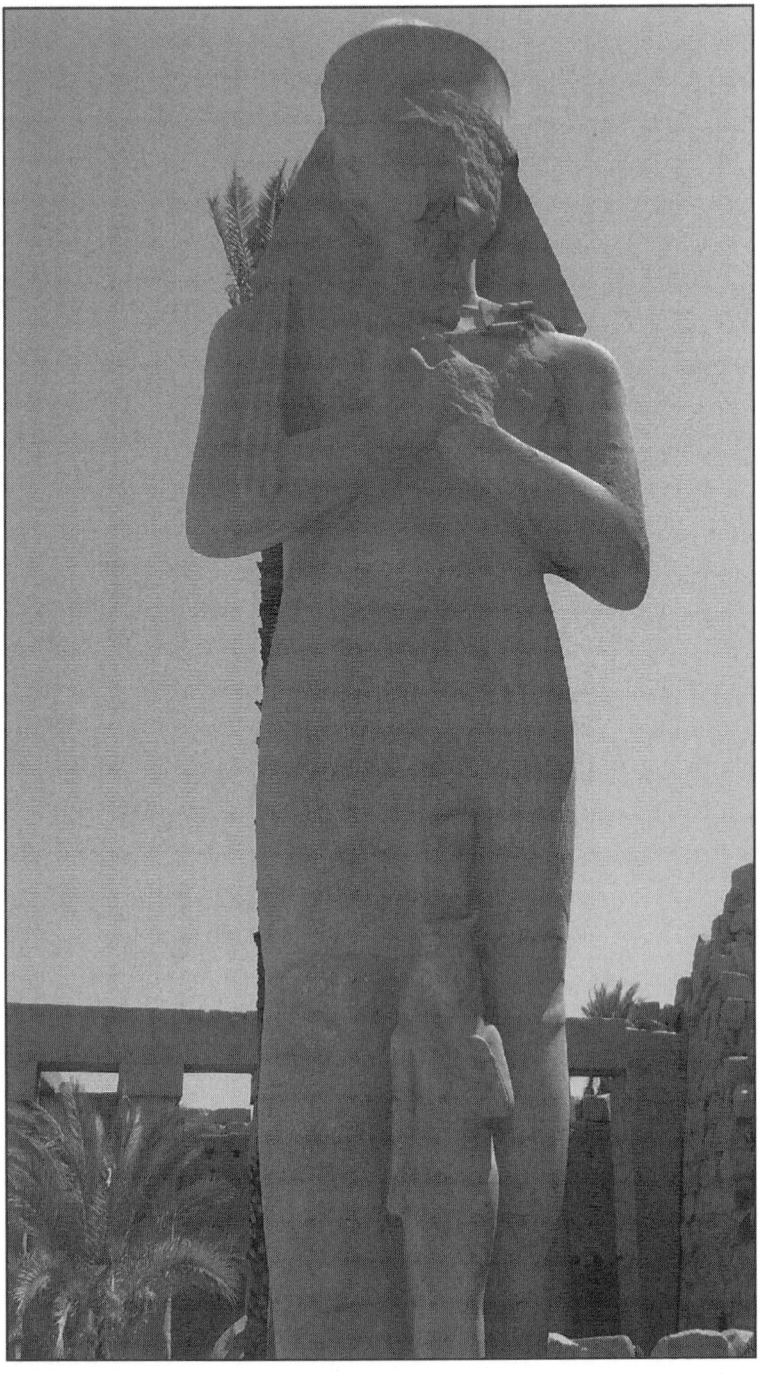

Tuesday 12th July

Optional early morning hot air balloon flight
Morning visit to Karnak Complex and Luxor Temple
Optional afternoon city tour of Luxor
by horse drawn carriage
Evening Egyptian dancing show

For those romantic souls who were taking the dawn balloon ride over Luxor, there was a £80 bill each and a 4am start. They would be back in time for breakfast! Not participating in that particular activity, our call came at 8am and we were off to our last official excursion – the Karnak Complex and Luxor Temple on the East Bank. There was much less hassle here. The traders were actually quite tame compared to our previous encounters. What a relief!

Karnak is truly enormous. Inside the beautifully cool entrance hall is a huge model of the area. The walls are hung with photographs showing scenes of excavations from the last 100 years or so. They even have the little train which took the archaeologists to the sites and returned filled up with rubble and sand from the excavations.

The entrance here, as wherever else we had been, had a metal detecting arch to walk through. Some beep, some don't.

No one seems to take any notice, whatever they do! Even the ship had one (which wasn't plugged in).

More and more treasures in Karnak are gradually being uncovered and restored. We took a long, hot walk across a 'boulevard' with young, shade-less trees – previously home to a small village which had been moved to open up the entire entrance area to the temple – guarded by the Avenue of Sphinxes. The complicated column arrangements and stunning statues, the obelisks and figures were awe-inspiring. They certainly saved the best until last. This is truly a fascinating monument.

A line is currently being excavated from Queen Hot Chicken Soup's temple on other side of river to Karnak and Luxor Temple, to find the extended Avenue of Sphinxes.

The vendors got us on the way back. I took Melody back to the coach as she was so tired, leaving the others to explore and take photos. We bagged a green stone cat and matching scarab for £2. This caused consternation to the vendor who wanted double, but having taken my money, and me having the goods in hand, it was stalemate. We walked away without further ado –

no commotion followed us – and we headed for the little shops to find a drink. In 40 degrees-plus of heat, even bargaining for cans of drink is stressful! Prices start around £5. You can usually get them down to £1.50. Here we actually managed to find a can of the illusive Ice Tea, much to Melody's delight. There's a little avenue of shops to the side of the entrance hall which you have to brave on your way out. A very understanding guard allowed us to 'go in through the out door' so we could avoid it.

With a plethora of temples under our belts, Philae was starting to look a bit like Kom Ombo and Habu like Edfu, or was that the other way around? We've seen so many wonderful and exciting things which I don't want to forget or have jumbled up in my memory. The hours I've spent on this book have been well worthwhile.

The papyrus shop. On the way to Luxor Temple (yes, another one to do yet), we were treated to a demonstration of how papyrus is made at a swish-looking papyrus shop. Surprisingly simple, the dark green skin is removed (which is strong and can be used to make sandals and hats), then the inside white stalk is sliced to the required length and soaked in water for six days, after which it is laid in a woven fashion to make the square of 'paper', then left to dry in a press for a further six days. Then, hey presto – a sheet of papyrus paper. To prove the fact, in true Blue Peter style, (you Brits will know what I mean), our jovial host produced 'one he had made earlier'!

A walk around the showrooms revealed the most stunning images and designs. Such vibrant colours and scenes illustrated on paintings of all shapes and sizes. Imagine the tombs and temples, the figures, the depicted stories all decorated with sumptuous depth and attention to detail. The staff were all polite and attentive, explaining the stories behind the pieces. Prices, I thought, were quite reasonable. LE75 for the smallest picture, up to around LE2500 for a 2m x 1m masterpiece – absolutely out of this world.

If an Egyptian-themed living or bedroom appeals to you, £250 for an amazing original art centrepiece seems like a good buy.

Deciding to save our Egyptian-themed living space for another day, we boarded the coach for Luxor Temple.

Luxor Temple is nowhere near as big or complex as Karnak. It is, nevertheless, pretty impressive, particularly with the Avenue of Sphinxes leading from it.

This is the only temple in Egypt that is not completely straight from front to back, there's a little kink in it.

Its history is particularly interesting. The temple has been used by various religious denominations over the years – ancient Egyptians, Romans, Christians, etc. In more recent times, around the 13th Century, after thousands of years of mud and sand building up, a famous Muslim, Sheikh Yusuf al-Haggag who helped the city, was given permission to build a mosque on the site. After modern-day excavation, the entrance to the still-standing mosque can be found a few metres above floor level in all its glory.

Here you will find the small grave in which Yousef Ibn Abdel-Raheem, (also known as Abu Al-Haggag), was buried.

Stiflingly hot, I retreated to the coach. Ken had been waiting there with Melody as she simply could not face another temple, and I took next watch so he could go and explore. Sitting in the cool coach we watched old men in white traditional Egyptian garb plying papyrus pictures, and armed guards sat in a portacabin opposite, chatting, while their mates brought them trays of hot, steaming coffee.

Little kids tried to sell us some bookmarks. "Only one pound, lady, Madame, only one pound, very good quality!"

graffiti

The evening horse-drawn carriage ride around Luxor city was fantastic. Good decision! It was a bit scary in places but supremely enjoyable overall.

Our coach dropped us just outside Luxor temple where the horses and carriages were waiting. Long faces were pulled when we insisted on all four of us going in one carriage. We were not getting split up, oh no! Had we known we would all go in convoy, it might have been different. The horse pulled us all with ease and the axle didn't split in two.

The ride took around an hour. We traversed main streets and back alleys, weaving around double-lane streets, side roads and mud paths. Riding down Television Street we saw 'western' style shops, Luxor street style, women's clothing, shoe shops, trendy men's wear – this has to be the Luxor version of Bond Street, complete with pot holes and beggars. Having said that, we were not particularly hassled. No one jumped on the carriages to try and sell us anything. A few starry-eyed children waved shyly, shopkeepers beckoned us to come into their shops, but nothing more sinister or threatening than that. We were, however, the objects of fascination.

Our white legs on show (don't wear shorts if you are going to take this ride and take a towel to sit on so you don't stick the plastic-covered seats) – oh là là! Ellen's blond hair was such an obvious attraction that she felt most uncomfortable, even with it tied up. At 15, to be the object of desire for practically every male we passed under 95 (and 90% of the pedestrians were male) was quite overwhelming for her.

At length, we turned into the souk, where it was darker, with a much heavier atmosphere, thanks to the coverings. How I wished I could have disguised myself as a local and walked through that market. It took about ten minutes to ride down from beginning to end. The sides of the carriages almost touched the thronging crowd. Teeming with early evening shoppers, we passed men ironing and mending shoes in the street. There were spice sellers with their aromatic baskets full of saffron and fennel and caraway seeds, coriander and fenugreek, fruit stalls with gigantic melons, bananas and grapes; brightly coloured scarves and dresses hung up everywhere. Chunks of meat hung from doorways wrapped in muslin and fresh bread and pastries gave off delicious aromas. It was difficult to hear yourself think above the hubbub of the bartering and the cries of greeting. Part of the market runs under an elevated road – the prime location for an illicit encounter, a surreptitious meeting or sheltered bench to sit on, smoke a nargila pipe and watch the bustling world go by.

We emerged from the market as the sun was beginning to set and the air seemed slightly cooler. It was the run-up to the Moulid of Abu el Haggag (festival), and revellers had dressed up in shiny hats and were dancing around the square in front of Luxor temple. Sweet stalls were being set up. The moulid lasts two days it takes place annually two weeks before the start of Ramadan.

Our young driver pointed out the railway station and temple – showing off the few English words he had learned.

Sorry that our ride had come to an end, we peeled ourselves off the seats, tipped the driver and boarded the coach back to the ship for dinner. There was a twirling dance show and disco planned for us tonight. Exhausted, we gave it a miss, deciding we'd wait for the video to come out.

It was our last night on board! We'd be disembarking the following morning. I abandoned the packing half way through, wondering where all this stuff had come from that I'd fitted into two suitcases before we left. We went to sleep, heads facing the air con outlet again, dismissing the remaining packing problem until the morning.

On board

OK, worst bit first - no loo roll down the loo. A special bin is provided. This, actually, did not turn out to be as bad as it seemed as the rooms were cleaned twice a day. There's a handy little 'mini shower' attached to the wall which can be used if any cleaning is needed after you've hit the 'evac' button. This may not be the case with all ships.

All the food prepared on board was washed with mineral water. Mineral water ice cubes were the order of the day! We were advised not to buy bottled water from street sellers (for obvious reasons).

Only clean your teeth with mineral water.

We had a fridge, hair dryer, safe and TV (which had films in English sometimes in the evenings) in our room.

If you have a fridge in the cupboard, pull it as far forward as you dare and leave the cupboard door open. The fridge will work much more efficiently and get colder as more air can get around the back of it.

Tip

There was absolutely no need whatsoever to take towels.

Karnak Complex

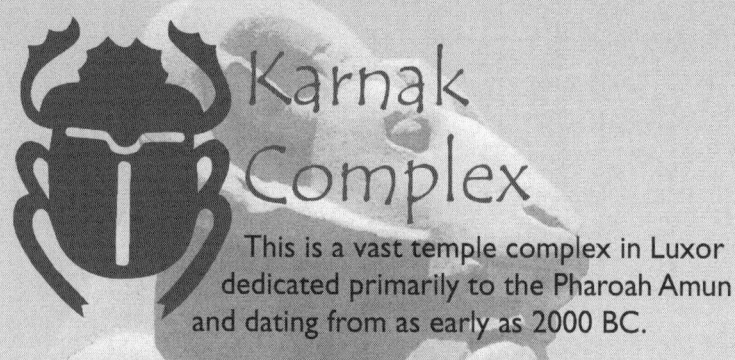

This is a vast temple complex in Luxor dedicated primarily to the Pharoah Amun and dating from as early as 2000 BC.

After a century of foreign occupation, the New Kingdom (1550-1150 BC) of Egypt emerged, with its capital at Thebes (Luxor). The capital city was embellished with grandiose temples worthy of the majesty of the pharaohs, the greatest being Karnak.

The temple complex was the centre of worship for Amun, his wife, Mut and their son, Khons. Each of them had a 'precinct' (area) in the temple complex, the greatest and largest belonging to Amun. There was also a precinct for Montu, the local falcon-headed god.

The complex covers a site almost a mile by two miles in area. There are over 25 temples and chapels in the complex, including separate shrines for the three boats that took the statues of the gods on their annual trip on the flooding Nile.

Sanctuaries, obelisks and groups of columns all feature accounts of the heroic deeds done by 30 or so successive pharaohs. Each one added a new temple, shrine, or pylon and carved detailed hieroglyphic inscriptions, which resulted in it reaching a size, complexity and diversity not seen elsewhere.

Construction at Karnak began in the 16th Century BC and continued into the Greco-Roman period – a staggering 1300 years of construction. Few of the individual features of Karnak are unique, but the sheer size and number of them makes it one of the most impressive temple complexes in Egypt.

When the pharaoh Akhenaton abandoned the traditional worship of Amun and took up worship of Aten, the sun god, he built a temple to Aten at Karnak. After his death, the Theban priests destroyed all signs of sun worship at Karnak and elsewhere.

The complex includes several of the finest examples of ancient Egyptian design and architecture. Amongst them are the Hypostyle Hall which covers an area of around 6,000 square metres. It is filled with 134 enormous pillars, the highest over 20m tall, and each about 13m around.

The most spectacular of the temples at Karnak is the Temple of Amun (Amun's Precinct), the only section open to the public. It is entered via the Avenue of Sphinxes, or Sacred Way, that once stretched the two miles from Karnak to Luxor Temple.

The Obelisk of Thutmose I, a 22m monument, is the only one of four original obelisks that is still standing.

Entrance price: adults LE65, children LE35

Luxor Temple

This is a great temple complex in modern Luxor dedicated to Amun, a creator god often fused with the sun-god Ra into Amun-Ra.

Construction work on the temple began during the reign of Amenhotep III in the 14th Century BC. Horemheb and Tutankhamun added columns, statues and friezes, and earlier, Akhenaten had obliterated his father's cartouches and installed a shrine to the Aten. Major expansion took place under Ramses II some 100 years after the first stones were put in place.

Each year, to ensure the flooding of the Nile that was necessary to national prosperity, the statues of Amun, Mut (goddess of war), and Khons (the moon god) were sailed down the river to Karnak for a great festival.

The temple fell into disrepair during the Late Period. Alexander the Great claimed to have undertaken major reconstruction work 'to restore it to the glory of Amenhotep's times' in the 320s BC. During Rome's domination of Egypt it was converted into a centre for the Roman emperor cult.

By the time of the Arab conquest, the temple was largely buried underneath accumulated river silt, to the extent that the Mosque of Abu Haggag was built on top of it in the 13th Century (much reworked since, but one of the minarets dates back to the original construction).

Luxor Temple is huge in scale — it once housed a village within its walls. It has several pylons (monumental gateways) that are some 65m long. The First Pylon is over 21m high, fronted by massive statues and several obelisks. There are numerous open areas, once used for various forms of worship but now empty. Later additions include a shrine to Alexander the Great, a Roman sanctuary and an Islamic shrine to a 13th Century holy man.

The entrance to the temple is from the north, where a causeway lined with sphinxes that once led all the way to Karnak begins. This road, known as the Sacred Way or Avenue of Sphinxes, was a later addition, dating from the time of Nectanebo I in the 30th Dynasty.

A cache of 26 New Kingdom statues was found under the floor in the inner sanctum area in 1989 – hidden away by pious priests, presumably, at some moment of internal upheaval or invasion. These splendid pieces are now on display at the nearby Luxor Museum.

Entrance price: adults LE50, children LE25

Cruising

A Nile cruise is a wonderful thing to do. I recommend checking that the ship you choose has all the facilities you would like, as there is a lot of cruising/docking, compared with the visits and excursions, particularly as in our case, when we were docked in Luxor. We were about 6 miles out of town, so a visit to anywhere necessitated a taxi. Not all allow children on board, some allow children over 12.

Unless you count the Isle of Wight ferry, I'm not a seasoned cruiser and so somewhat unqualified to judge. However, if you are only interested in cruising, stick with the Med or the Caribbean. Other guests were complaining, unfairly I thought, that our trip did not compare favourably with a Caribbean cruise. My guess is that it could not possibly compare, no matter what your criteria – neither favourably nor unfavourably. It has to be your proverbial chalk and cheese!

Tip

If you want to cruise and see the sights, book the full excursion package in advance and budget for a couple the optional excursions. The Nubian village trip to see the crocodiles with the camel ride and the horse-drawn carriage ride around Luxor both really added to our experience. Others may prefer the Abu Simbel trip or the sound and light show at Luxor.

If you just want to see the sights, then staying in Luxor is not a bad option.

Karnak, Luxor and Habu Temples pretty much top the others we saw, plus you are free to visit the Valley of the Kings and the Valley of the Queens at leisure (even Queen Hot Chicken Soup's Mortuary Temple). You would have any number of perfume factories, alabaster and papyrus shops on hand. Gold and silver jewellers are not in short supply – plus there's the covered souk which would probably take you a day or so to wander up and down. Other must-sees include the Museum of Mummification and the Winter Garden Hotel terraces where you can take tea and watch the sunset and the river go by.

If you are peckish and not keen on the local dishes, we saw MacDonald's and Pizza Hut on top of each other (unfortunately the photo was too out of focus to print)! Another bonus for Luxor, it's not that far from the airport and taxis are as cheap as chips.

Lunch Menu

Chicken soup (hot!)

Rice

'Blankets'
(we got braised beef cubes which were very nice but didn't look much like blankets)

Boiled vegetables

Fresh fruit and crème caramel slices

This meal was part silver service, part buffet

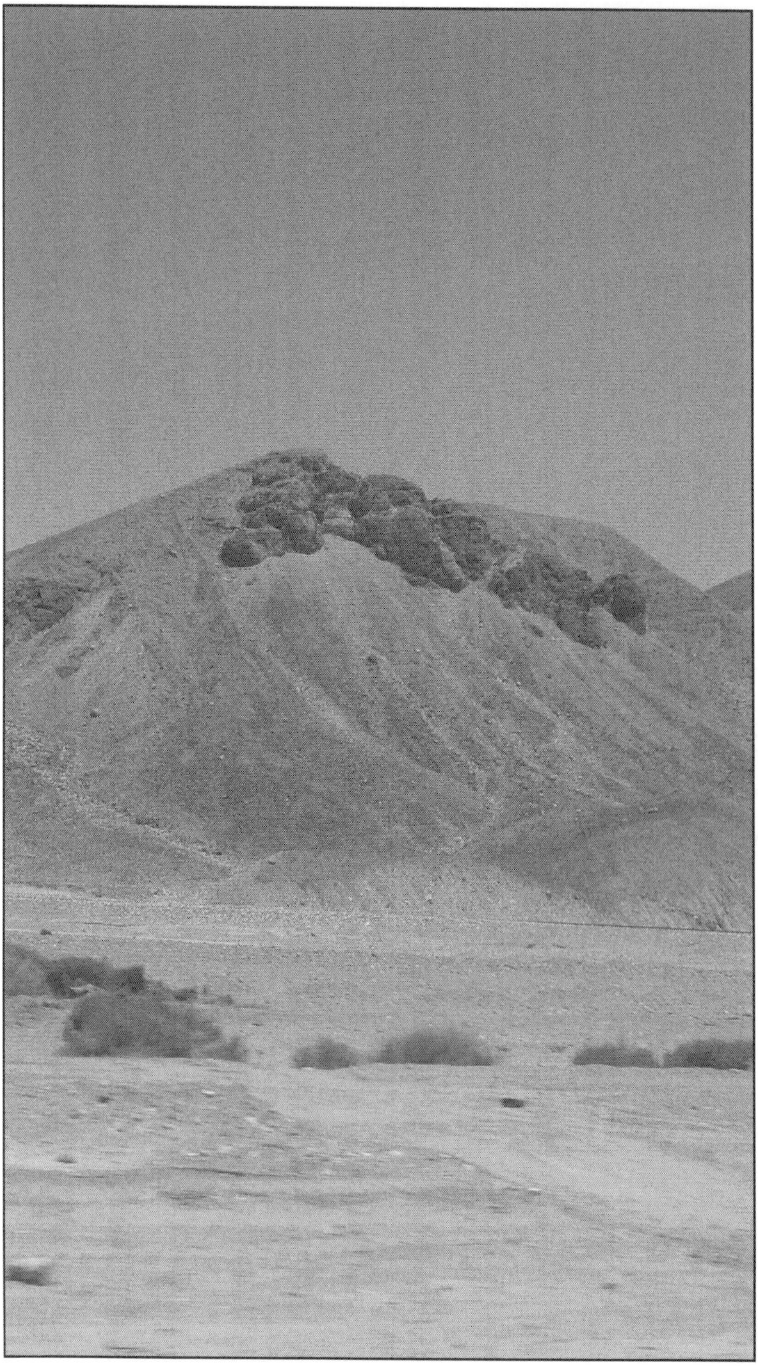

A	H	N	U
B	I	O	V
C or	J	P	W
D	K	Q	X
E or or		R	Y or
F	L	S	Z
G	M	T	SH

Wednesday 13th July

Morning taxi ride from Luxor to Hurghada
Afternoon in the Titanic Palace Hotel, Hurghada

Morning arrived all too soon and, yes, we managed to pack all the heavies (marble cats, scarabs) and breakables carefully into one case, which we would 'try' not to open until we got home, cramming everything else into the other. Fat chance of that! At breakfast our table-mates who had occupied the top floor cabin at the front, above the bar (the only one with fully-working air conditioning, who were sleeping under blankets), looked a bit weary, to say the least. Not only had they been up at 3.30 the previous morning for their hot air balloon ride (which they heartily enthused about, despite being scared of heights), last night's disco was so loud, their cabin floor was shaking! Eventually they went down to complain and were aghast to find only four people in the bar – there could hardly have been any objection to turning the music down a touch.

Our private taxi for our transfer to Hurghada arrived early at around 9.30am. We said our good-byes and see-you-theres as many of the guests were also going to Hurghada for some well-earned R 'n' R – a few by taxi, others by coach. We gave additional tips to those we felt deserved it, on top of the £15 each passenger had already given as a general ship's tip which was to be shared out among all the staff.

Now for a road trip with a difference! Our taxi was, in fact, a mini bus which was easily big enough for the four of us, our luggage and then some. Our driver, Hannay, was the ultimate chauffeur. A very accomplished driver, he was well-used to the hustle and bustle and vying for position on the Egyptian road system.

Jostling our way out of Luxor was interesting, to say the least. In the town you find police check points every 200m or so. Not all are manned. The idea of the 'convoy' really doesn't exist anymore, it is every driver for himself, but the check points remain. They consist of metal barriers or giant painted oil cans, positioned half way across each lane, forming a chicane around which everyone is funnelled into. An amazing number of vehicles of varying sizes and methods of propulsion seemed to be able to navigate the chicanes at any given time, speeding up and slowing down to negotiate the huge road humps either side which dictate a top speed of 5 kph. I lost count of the number of red traffic lights we drove through. I've no idea why they were there, as no one took a blind bit of notice of them.

As the scenery sped by, we saw mud huts, old buildings and a sugar beet factory. Either side of the road were irrigation canals, allowing the farmers up to five crops per year from the fertile land.

Melody wasn't on top form, but recovered enough after a five minute stop on the roadside to finally fall asleep on our laps.

Egyptian city life morphed into a rural backdrop, which in turn rolled into to desert landscape. The hot desert sands loomed either side of us with a big, long, tarmac road stretching straight in front for as far as the eye could see, disappearing into a tiny point who knows how far away. The road, it turned out, was not as smooth and straight as it first appeared, as Hannay must have known very well. Large sections of it were in fairly bad repair, not surprising given the weather conditions. Sixty per cent of the journey was spent driving on the 'wrong' side of the road to avoid the pot holes and bumpy surface. Whenever there was an oncoming vehicle, we temporarily switched sides – quite a difference in ride quality!

The sand became stones. The stones became mounds and the mounds became hills of stone and sand then, after two hours, we pulled in to a roadside café for a Coke and to eat the chicken sandwiches (left those, actually, worried they were too warm), cheese rolls, crisps and apples which had very thoughtfully been handed to us for our journey as we'd left the ship. Stepping out of the taxi, we were blasted by hot wind of 42 degrees C and headed gratefully for the shaded area of the café.

The owners didn't mind us eating our own food there. We did admire the items they were selling (usual scarves, dresses and trinkets) and availed ourselves of their facilities – having to drop coins into a specially constructed, lop-sided box at the entrance, with an attendant rushing over to make sure we'd dropped the appropriate amount in. Egyptian pound coins look very much like their English or European equivalent – as long it is small, gold and round, any coin would do.

Back in our taxi, we were looking forward to arriving. 40 minutes later, the desert almost disappeared and we could see the hazy Red Sea in the distance. "Hurghada very nice," our driver announced. "Ten degrees cooler than Luxor." Phew! "Hurghada big. 420 hotels. Town to left, five hotels, very nice. Town to right, three hotels, also very nice." Erm, maybe we chose the wrong resort? Three hotels sounds infinitely preferable than 420 to me!

Entering Hurghada, the hotel exteriors were pretty impressive. Hannay drew our attention to the shipping 'malls'. "Here shopping," he said, "Here shopping also." (Obviously the thing to do here.) He'd done an excellent job getting us here and we thanked him, shook hands and handed him his tip as he unloaded our cases from the taxi.

Long journey, but one I am glad to have made.

There are three Titanic hotels in Hurghada. Ours was the Titanic Beach, on an all-inclusive basis. This, indeed, is a grand hotel of Titanic proportions and grandeur. The perceived opulence in the reception areas is obscene when compared to the little mud huts and donkey-drawn carriage life-style of the Egyptian folk we had passed on the way.

Generally, I guess that most of the big hotels here would offer the same service and standards/ facilities as this one.

It transpired that we'd been transferred to the Titanic Palace hotel which is really part of the original (but closer to the beach and less busy). Having been fitted with our ID bracelets, Ken and the girls headed off to one of the many pools to cool down and I had a quick rekey around the hotel while Reception tried to find us two interconnecting rooms rather than the two standard rooms they'd originally allocated us.

After 15 minutes they came up trumps and the porter trollied our luggage with me in tow. The rooms were quite big and well kitted out. The beds were enormous (even the singles) and very comfortable. The twin room the girls had was lovely and cold. Guess what? The air con in the adult's room wasn't working properly. We hoped that if we left the interconnecting door open, the icy wafts would find their way through — sadly this was not the case. We did ask for someone to come and fix it the following day, and they didn't turn up. But hey! The fridge was stocked with Coke, Fanta and mineral water, had space for wine, and there was a safe and a big flat screen TV in each room. We had a great balcony overlooking the pools.

The bathrooms were decked out in floor-to-ceiling marble with a great walk-in shower big enough for a party, complete with washing line, and, there was no problem with loo paper!

Not everyone had a hotel room. Here you can rent little 'bungalows' which are in the middle of a pool and have their own little ladders down into the water. How cute!

This is a huge pool complex with the greenest, springiest grass I have ever walked on and sun beds galore. The waterslide area near the beach with slides suitable for most ages is very popular. Some you just slide down, others you whizz down on boats or mats, the big blue one is like a half pipe – you slide down one side and ascend up the other almost to the top (depending on how much you weigh) – really scary! There's a lazy river to paddle around, a pirate ship with six slides for the little ones and a wave pool.

We exchanged our towel cards for towels and after the girls had done a few of the slides, we wandered on to the beach. It's nice sand with thatched umbrellas and windbreaks shading rows and rows of sun loungers. The tide was in. The sea is about 20cm deep for about 1km – easily heated by the sun, it was warmer than the pools. The fish swimming around were fascinating, as were the small milky-white jelly fish with light purple heart-shaped markings in their middles.

We were assured there was nothing harmful in the water (except for the sharks a bit further out!), including the long, black-tentacled spider starfishes who crawled up our arms and tickled us. We spent an enjoyable afternoon exploring the beach.

Dinner was a buffet affair in the main restaurant. This restaurant was open and airy. There were no queues for the food and there was plenty to choose from.

We were hoping for a bottle of wine to take to our room for the evening. This unfortunately wasn't covered by the all-inclusive deal – only glasses of wine were allowed – OK, let's beat the system! We collected as many glass-fulls as we could carry and sneaked them back to the fridge in our room. If you collect the larger plastic containers, it means fewer trips!

After the buzzing bug-killing super sprayer machine went past our door, we sent Ellen down to get a couple more! Ha!

The girls went to sleep in their nice, cold room. We survived, though, it wasn't that bad! There was even an English film on TV to watch.

Obviously, if you don't have worn out kids with you, you'd be out partying the night away and sleep all morning. No such luxuries for us!

Hotel Menu

Salad buffet with many different dishes to choose from, chopped vegetables to pulses, stuffed vine leaves, pasta salad, with and without dressing

Soup and a variety of different bread and rolls

Hot dishes of chicken and fish, a variety of cooked vegetables and potatoes, rice

Pasta and choice of sauces

A nightly carvery bar with a selected meat

Outdoor barbeque with a selected meat

A big choice of puddings and cakes

Help yourself to drinks, soft and alcoholic

Thursday 14th July

Day in the hotel at Hurghada

The next morning we hit the main restaurant again for breakfast. We found a great selection of bread, toast, yoghurt, cereal, cold meat and cheese and, of course, tea and coffee. All very civilised!

We decided to go snorkelling to see the wonderfully coloured fish and reef we had been hearing about. It was a bit of a shock to find the tide out quite so far (about a kilometre, I'd say) but the walk out to it in the little rivers of warm water which trickled around stones and sandbanks was superbly interesting. The spider starfish were there, crawling out of their little holes as the water crept over them and the other little marine creatures which hid not far below the surface.

The water gradually became a little deeper. Glistening fish darted this way and that. Spiky coal-black anemones were attached to rocks and flashes of bright turquoise were visible just under the water.

At the end of the shallow plateau, the sea bed dropped away sharply to reveal a small reef teeming with sea life – blue and gold striped fish, silver ones, thin ones, fat ones...

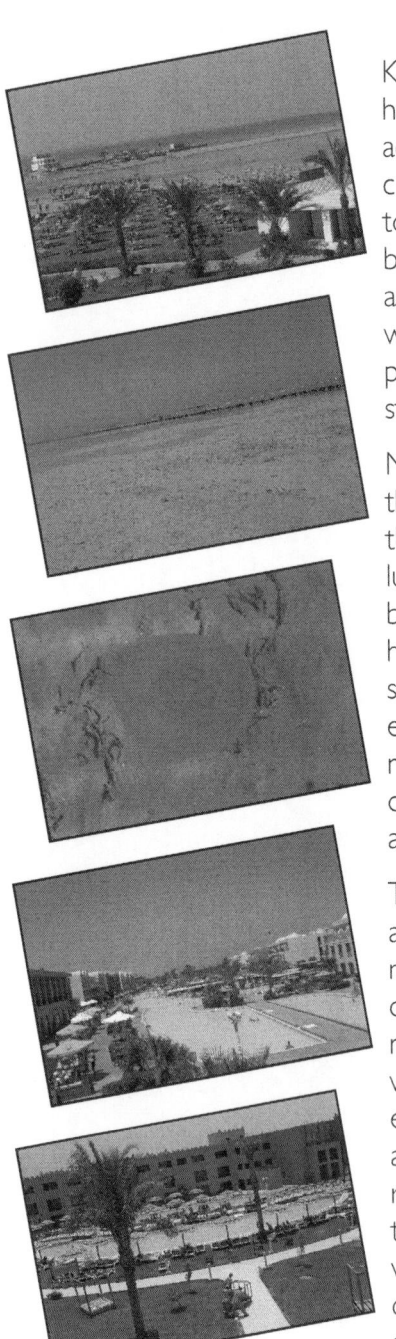

Ken and the girls snorkelled happily, exploring the hidden aquatic treasures. At length they climbed the ladder up to the jetty to make the return journey to the beach on 'dry land'. I heard shouts as they passed me – I'd very slowly waded back towards the shore, poking around the underwater stones and taking photographs.

Most people seemed to be availing themselves of the snacks, rather than going to the restaurant for lunch. The pool bar and the beach bar were serving hamburgers, hotdogs and chips. With ever-so-slightly-dodgy tummies (not everything here is washed in mineral water, that's for sure), we decided to give the 'snacks' a miss and headed for the main restaurant.

The menu was exactly the same as dinner had been the previous night... No, I'm not kidding! It turned out that every lunch and evening meal served in the main restaurant was, yes, exactly the same. In the evenings, they do have a carvery and barbecue going outside the restaurant. We had had what we thought were quail last night. Oh well! If you were disciplined, you could probably avoid eating the same thing three or four days in a row.

Not to be caught out, we started our wine collection early, taking a couple of glasses up to put in the fridge for later!

By the time we reached the waterslide area, ALL the sun beds had been reserved, mainly, it turned out, by the staff who would 'sell' you one for a quick baqsheesh. Saves getting up at 6am to beat the Germans, at least! The hotel boasts a whole 'sales' team who wander around offering massages, kite surfing lessons, plaited hair-dos and henna tattooing – a sort of equivalent to the street vendors of Luxor in uniform, only much nicer! Ken and the girls did some of the slides and we had fun jumping up and down in the wave pool. It was pretty hot, still, and I was very glad of the thatched, shade-giving umbrellas everywhere.

The pools close at 6pm for chemical cleaning so – everybody out! After a shower and a little rest, we decided to explore the hotel and make arrangements for our pick up the following day. This turned out to be rather more complicated than we'd expected as the hotel staff themselves were not responsible. We had to call a number and arrange it over the phone with some poor chap who's English was a bit rocky, to say the least. Even a meeting with our 'holiday rep' didn't help much. Why we needed one of those when we were only there for two days was beyond me. Eventually, it was settled that we would be picked up at 2pm from the Titanic Beach reception and the porters would collect our luggage from our room at 11am.

Our explorations that evening took us up the escalator next to the main restaurant in the Titanic Palace side of the hotel. At the top were huge lounge areas with sofas, tables and a bar. In the connecting corridor to the Titanic Beach we found the games room (Entertainment Centre, as they call it), complete with four-lane bowling alley, pool tables of varying sizes, table football, video games machines and computers with internet access for those with Facebook withdrawal symptoms. To use any of these facilities, you have to buy tokens. Next door was the entrance to the nightclub. There's even a shopping arcade selling just about everything we'd spent the last week bargaining for – all the usual tourist souvenirs and even a little supermarket. The shopkeepers stood in the doorways, encouraging us to enter. There was a carpet-maker demonstrating the art of weaving and an artist making stunning charcoal portraits from photographs. A special photography service would take a romantic picture of you and your beau at sunset and there were numerous spa treatments available to those who fancied them.

At the foot of the grand white staircase were more intimate restaurants offering international cuisine – all with hardly any diners in. To use these restaurants, you must stay at least one week and are then entitled to reserve places in any two of them in that week. Tough for us, then! We even saw a signpost to a ballroom!

Finding ourselves on the Titanic Beach side of the hotel, we decided to eat in the main restaurant there. It was pretty much the same as the Titanic Palace side, maybe slightly busier with a small children's section and Egyptian-style entertainment. A band of musicians walked around the diners singing and playing instruments and the whole place was livened-up with colourful hangings on the ceilings.

The rest of the evening's wine supply in hand, we walked the long walk back to our room, where the girls collapsed with fatigue (in their lovely cold room) and finally fell asleep.

Titanic Palace Hotel bathroom

Standing in front of the mirror, I had the distinct impression that the floor was moving, ever-so-slightly! It took several days for this sensation to subside

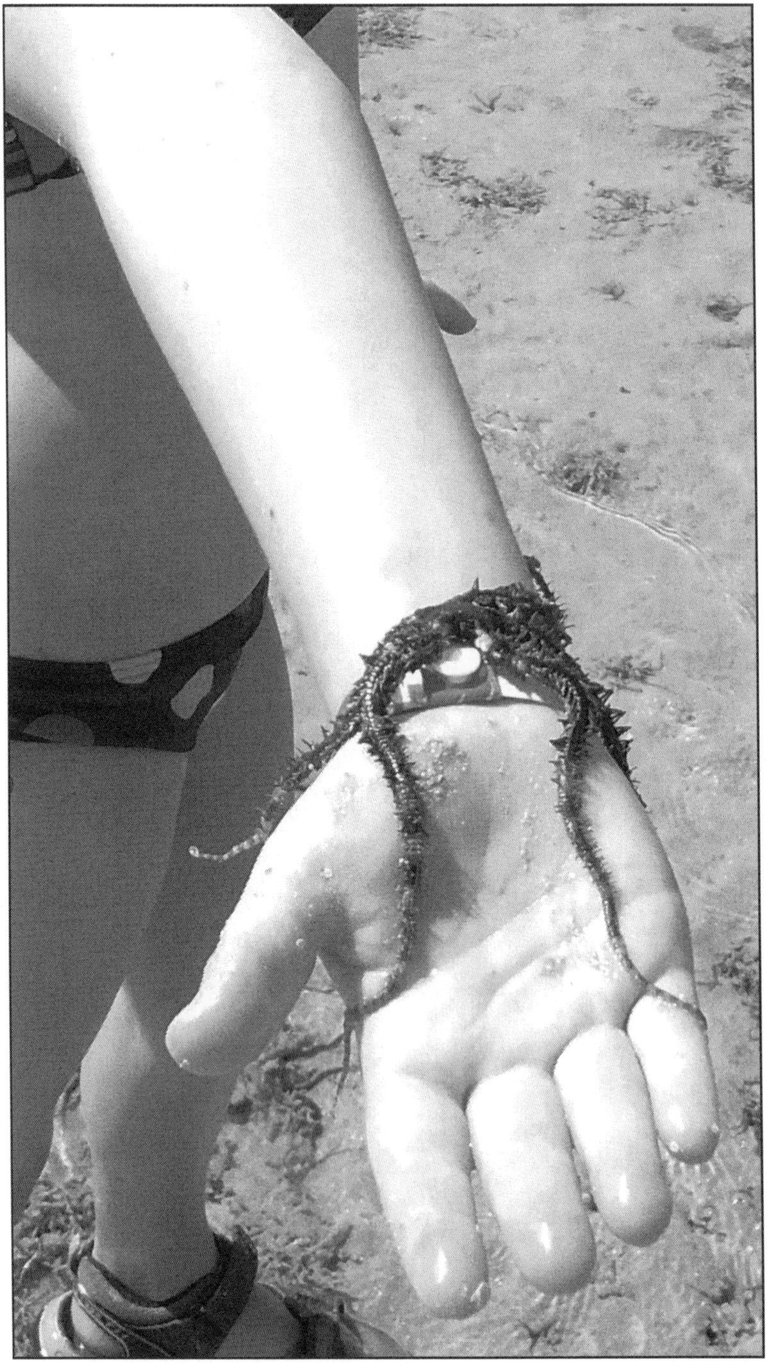

Friday 15th July

Travel day from Hurghada to Gatwick

So much for not unpacking one of the cases! That was never going to work. I'd put things in there I decided I needed and had left things out I really didn't need, of course! So after breakfast the entire two cases were repacked ready for our journey home. We'd planned a morning by the pool and had left out a change of clothes and space in the hand luggage (plus a plastic bag!) for our swimming gear.

We watched the morning stretching session, followed by the belly-dancing lessons held by the pool bar (I was dying to join in) and the aqua-aerobics course just afterwards.

Back at the room to meet the porter at the allotted time, he was nowhere to be seen! At 11.15am I called reception and miraculously there was a knock at the door! They insisted on leaving our luggage in the Titanic Palace reception until it was time to leave, when they would push it all the way to the other side of the hotel.

We messed around in the pool then, after a leisurely lunch, got changed in the rest rooms, handed back our towel cards and went to retrieve our luggage.

Main hotel facilities

Main buffet restaurant
Breakfast 07h00-10h00. Lunch 12h30-14h30
Dinner 18h30-21h.00 Late dinner 22h30-00h00

Beach restaurant
(Late lunch snacks) 12h30-16h00

À la carte restaurants
18h30-22h00
Indian, Japanese and Chinese, Fish, Mexican, Italian, Oriental

Pool Bar
Serves drinks from 10h00-23h00
Late continental breakfast 10h00-12h00
Snacks 13h00-17h00
Tea time 17h00-18h30 (Summer) 15h30-17h00 (Winter)

Cesar Bar and Pirates Lobby Bar
Open 24 hours serving all local spirits
Late snacks 00h00-07h00. Tea time 17h00-18h30

Captain Smith Bar
Open 18h30-22h00 serving all local spirits

Captain Inn Bar
10h00-00h00

Oasis Pool Bar and Sailors Beach Bar
10h00-sunset

Waves Disco Bar
22h00-02h00

Aqua Park open 10h00-17h00 (18h00 in Summer)
Entertainment Centre 10h00-01h00
Bowling alley, pool tables, internet access
Tennis and Mini Golf 08h00-17h00
Kids' Club 7 days per week 10h15-12h30 and 15h15-17h30

Waiting in the Titanic Beach reception for our lift, the hotel manager approached us and asked what we'd thought of the hotel. He asked us to recommend it on a website and handed me a card. They would dearly love to attract more English and French-speaking visitors, or Europeans in general.

I told him that I thought the hotel itself was lovely but, if I was honest, I'd found some of our fellow guests to be less than amiable. The majority of them appear to have been Russian and more than once I'd heard "Beer" or "Burger" at the bars without so much as a please or thank you. People had crashed into us without apologising or even acknowledging what they'd done and, overall, their unfriendliness had been a bit off-putting. The manager acknowledged that this was, indeed, a slight problem and said that if we'd informed him about it, he would have arranged for us to eat in one of the more quieter restaurants! If only we had known – next time I'll try this out and see if it works! We thanked him and left for the airport in the mini bus that had just arrived to collect us.

Hurghada airport is only a 15 minute ride away – over the proverbial speed humps. Entering the large, modern and cool building, our bags went through the x-ray machines right at the entrance. The requisite 'liquids in plastic bag' rule wasn't applied here at all. I probably could have got away with taking my water bottle through and thoroughly regretted throwing it in the green bin!

After passport control, the departure lounge was lined with souvenir shops, each one piled high with all the traditional 'artefacts'. The goods on sale seemed pretty reasonably priced (which cannot be said for the cans of drink, as with all airports). They had price tags attached, although you could still bargain. Imagine the T-shirts, 'jewel'-encrusted camels and elephants. See-through plastic pyramids with gold glitter in instead of snow to make a sand storm when you shook them. Wooden crocodiles, perfume bottles, designer handbag replicas in best plastic, scary wooden face masks, various miscellaneous items labelled 'made in Taiwan' and brightly painted boxes – you name it, it was there. "Very good price, Madame. I give you special discount for your beautiful daughter." Here we go again! The hassle here was minimal and we passed an enjoyable time wandering around the stands while we were waiting for our flight.

Besides the little kiosks selling canned drinks and sandwiches, there's a café and a Burger King with a play area for children. It's not a huge airport, but plenty big enough for the number of travellers at the time we were there.

We were bussed to the plane. Ken has Speedy Boarding so he went first and saved us seats together, with permission from the staff! We waved goodbye to the intense heat and to Egypt and looked forward to landing in the rainy UK after a five-and-a-half hour flight. We survived on Easyjet bacon rolls and some bread and biscuits I'd 'stolen' from the restaurant at lunch time.

It was indeed raining when we arrived back into North Terminal at Gatwick. I was too tired to notice how much it had been improved. We were 10 minutes too late to get the hire car from that terminal, grrr, so we hopped on the shuttle to the South Terminal and, seeing all our luggage, the very helpful guy at the desk took pity and gave us a much bigger hire car than we'd booked.

There was hardly any traffic on the motorway and we arrived at our destination just after midnight. The girls were thoroughly exhausted and after big hugs with their granddad, aunt and cousin, we all fell gratefully into bed.

The next two days we spent doing a bit of shopping and visiting relatives and on Monday morning, we reluctantly returned to Gatwick Airport.

The flight to Geneva took off and landed without incident – we were home!

"Where are we going on holiday next year, Mum?" asked the girls together...

Towel Sculptures

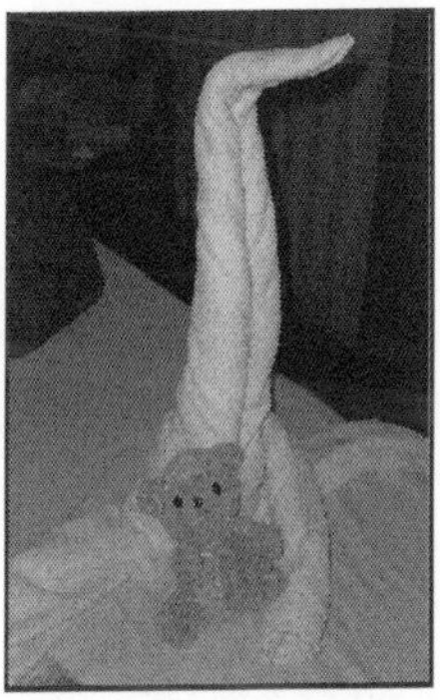
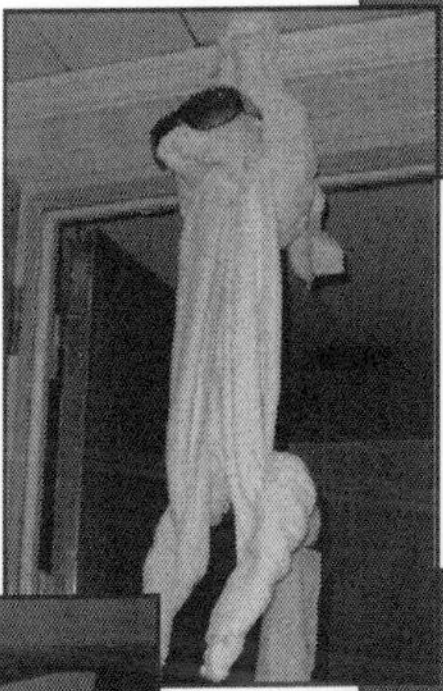
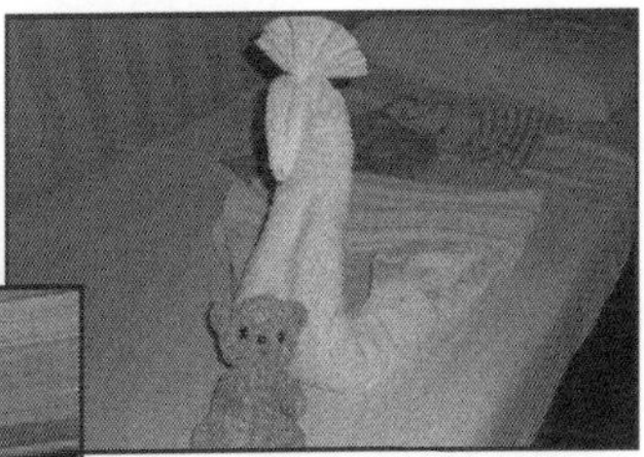
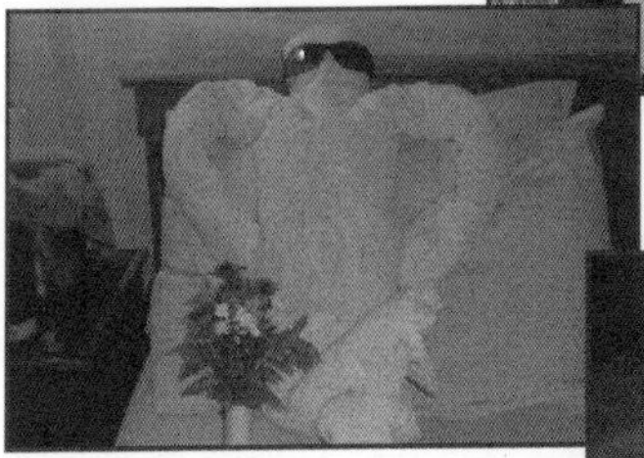
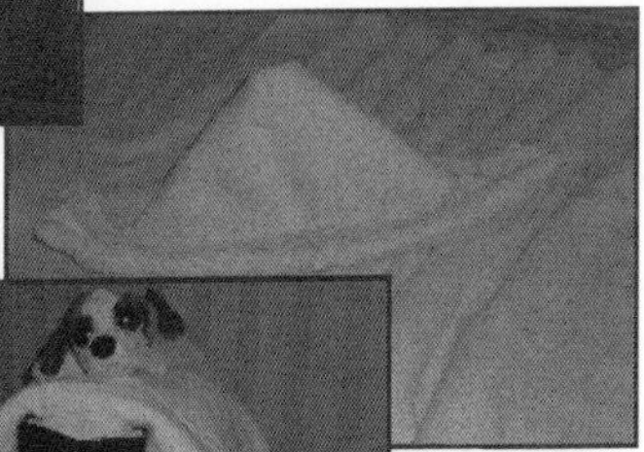
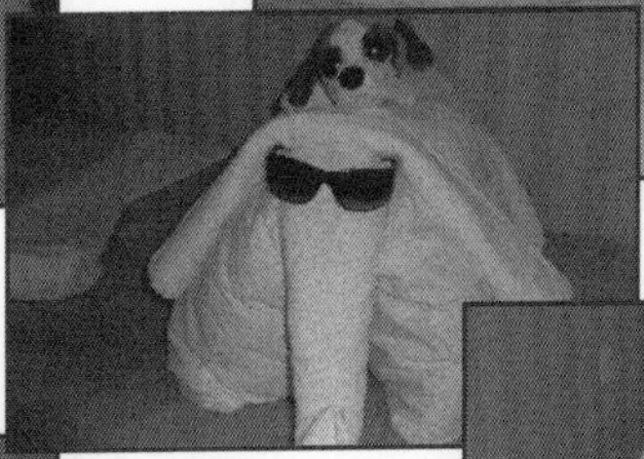
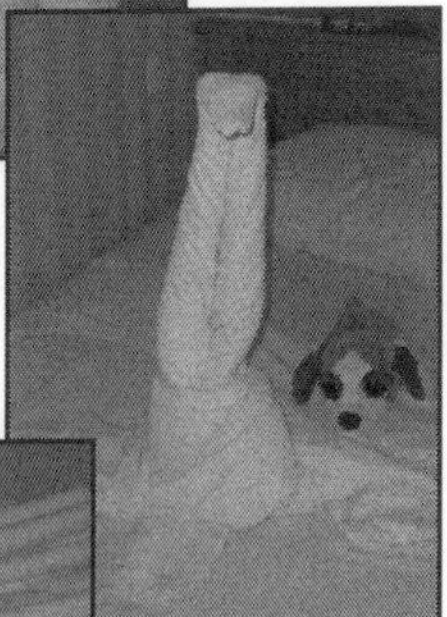
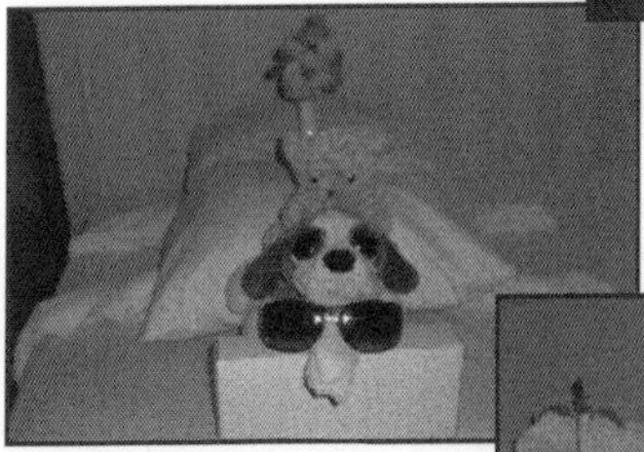
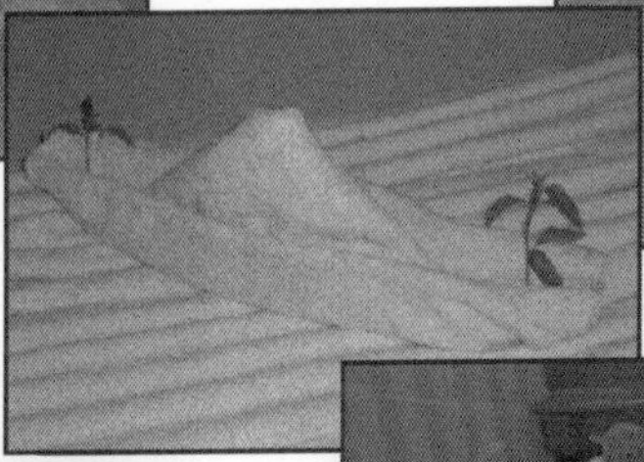
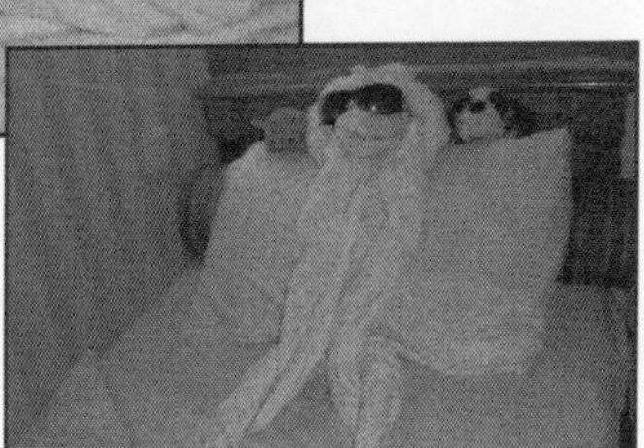
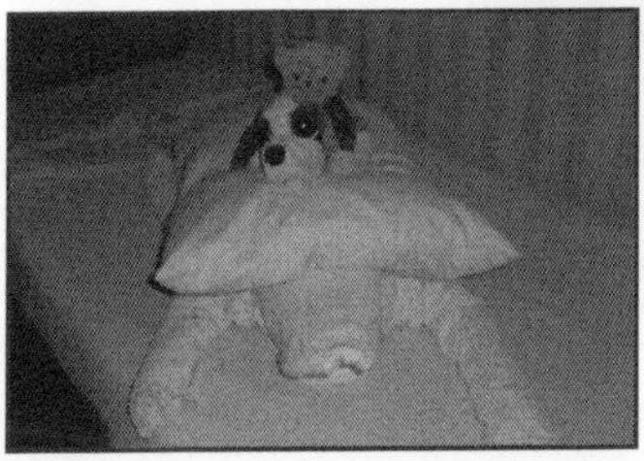

Useful Arabic words

(I can't testify to the spelling)

Please	Men fadlak
Thank you	Shoukran
Hi	Salam alykom
Good morning	Sabah el-kheir
Good evening	Messa el-kaeir
Good night	Tesbah ala-kaeir
OK, OK	Mashi mashi
Egyptian	Masry
Egypt	Misr
Pound	Genah
Piaster	Kerish
Tea	Shay
Coffee	Kahwa
Bread	Aish
Yes	Aiwa
No	Laa
How much	Bekam
Let's go	Yala bena
Go away	Emshy
My beloved	Habibi
Welcome	Ahlan wa-sahlan

Acknowledgements

I found some of the most interesting and useful history of the monuments on www.sacred-destinations.com, and other references on Wikipedia and Wikitravel.

Thanks to www.claseshistoria.com for allowing me to use some of your images.

I could give a long list of friends and family who have put up with me and helped me during the compilation of this book, but that's just too mushy. They know who they are. Thanks a lot, guys!

'Tubular Bells' is an album by Mike Oldfield, released in 1973.

All trademarks are recognised.

Look out for...

My next project will be a (much smaller) book on my personal experience of laser eye surgery – just in case you are thinking of having it done!

References

We booked our entire package through:
www.flightsandpackages.com

The companies they used are as follows:

Flights
www.easyjet.com

Nile cruise
www.youtravel.com

Transfers
www.a2btransfers.com

Hotel in Hurghada
www.bedswithease.com

About the author

Kim Molyneaux (pronounced moly-no) spent 20 years working in UK-based graphic design studios, specialising in typesetting and artwork. She upped-sticks and moved to the Swiss Romande, the beautiful French-speaking part of Switzerland, where she has lived for the last 10 years.

Kim now works freelance, producing artwork for PoD books (amongst other things) and as a virtual assistant and small business manager.

www.kimmolyneaux.com

Printed in Great Britain
by Amazon.co.uk, Ltd.,
Marston Gate.